EXPERIMENT WITH GOD

Show Up and See What Happens

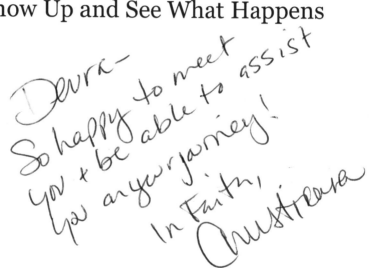

Devra —
So happy to meet
you + be able to assist
you on your journey!
In Faith,
Christiana

Christiana Carter

ISBN-13: 978-1542580342
ISBN-10: 154258034X

Published by:
10-10-10 Publishing
Markham, ON
Canada

Editor's Note
The names, details and circumstances may have been changed to protect the privacy of those mentioned in this publication.

He was always gentle, kind and loving. Remember if it's not, it's not of God.
- Your critic is NOT allowed!

Day 1 – Complete the 3 steps

Day 2 – Complete the 3 steps, and read Day 1

Day 3 – Complete the 3 steps, read Day 1 & 2

Day 4-30 – Repeat and keep going, read all the previous day's answers to the following questions. It's important to do this process every day without fail for 30 days.

It's really as simple as that. This process requires commitment, and the further you get into it the more time-consuming it will become. The more you write, the more you'll read, and by the end of the experiment you'll have engrained a new script for your life. Your time commitment will grow the more you write. So make space for that in your life as you continue with the process. It's important as it's re-writing the script of your life for new possibilities to show up.

Steps explained in more detail:

Step 1: Taking Stock
I've heard it said that we should make a grateful list. That's not a new concept. However, if I'm being honest, when I would sit down to make my list from this place of struggle, I wasn't feeling all that grateful. I was barely getting by.

I'm usually more grateful for things in the absence of them. Doing my grateful list at that time was about getting on the other side; my little voice would say, you really aren't grateful for your health until you are sick. That voice would be beat me up, working against me. Ever have that experience?

Instructions

This is a 30-day process. Complete the following steps each day and then re-read your previous entries in full to start imprinting your new script:

Step 1: Taking stock of your life in bullet point format
- What makes your heart open?
- What brings a smile to your face?
- What moments take your breath away? (This can be past or present.)
- It's okay to repeat items or themes; it's whatever comes to mind in the moment.

Step 2: What is God's belief system?
- What would God believe to be true if he was living your life?
- What would God's beliefs be?
- Again it's okay to repeat themes or beliefs; just write what comes to mind.

Step 3: What is God's vision for your life?
- What would God say you are supposed to do, or thinks you are capable of?
- What does God want to say to you? After a while these became conversations as you'll see, more of a dialogue.
- Write whatever comes to mind that God would say about you or to you. He is always out for your highest good no matter what. He doesn't see the bad, negative or any of our drama. Whatever you believe God to be, show up and do your best.
- In my experience, when I was resisting the process, God would address how I was feeling and speak into my fears or resistance.

all my own expenses to continue to do what I loved. I will be forever grateful for T. Harv Eker.

He took away the opportunity, and I had to show up and fight to be on stage. He wanted to see what I was made of; would I sink or rise to the challenge? If it wasn't for this Experiment, it's safe to say I would not have risen to the challenge.

After the completion of this Experiment, T. Harv saw me at my next event. Not only did he note significant improvement--I could show up, hold and command a room—but he offered to pay me again to do what I loved. This Experiment showed me my own power, and the power that comes from having a deep connected relationship with God.

Every part of my life got better; my anxiety dissipated, my relationships improved, I became more visible in my life and I started achieving what I set my mind to.

You have such a bright future. There is so much good in you and you have something of value to share with the world, your community or family. I have seen the blessings come into my life and I want that for you too.

"Well, I have been praying about my situation and the only message I keep getting back is, 'Why don't you live my vision of your life for 30 days? Why don't you believe what I believe to be true about you for the 30 days?'"

She stopped and looked at me, not saying a word at first, then she said, "That isn't a small thing! That's a big deal! It looks like the stakes are going up for you not listening. Do you need to break a leg before you take action?" I was caught. There was no way to ignore the message coming through. He even sent someone to point it out since I was avoiding listening. After sitting with the question for a while, I answered, "No. I'll do it. I get it!"

I've heard the old adage, God will whisper in your ear, tap you on the shoulder, punch you in the face or hit you with a bus. You choose when to listen to the message.

Here I was stuck with limited motion, unable to work; so I said, "Okay, I have nothing to lose." My mindset was really poor; even though I was reading positive things, in my heart I just didn't believe them. So it felt like a welcomed relief when I could take a vacation from myself and believe God's vision of me, and what he would believe to be true for me.

There is something magical having someone believe in the best in me. It's happened several times over my life during important crossroads. Except this time, the message was coming from inside me and I no longer had to look outside myself for the answers.

At that time, I had the opportunity to be an Assistant Trainer for Peak Potentials Training Company. T. Harv Eker was the owner of the company and, after seeing me on stage at three events, he didn't think I was strong enough to hold a room full of people. He was right. I was wounded and not owning my power or presence on stage. They stopped paying me. I had to pay out of pocket to be at events, cover

Have you ever found yourself repeating patterns and getting frustrated? Have you ever struggled to keep your mind right so you could attract the life you want? Me too!

I've been to so many seminars, workshops, trainings. So many leaders say to fake it until you make it; live as if, the power of positive thinking, affirmations, writing visions or goals and reading them daily. I've heard so many different variations.

The key that kept tripping me up is that I was ultimately responsible for the outcome. If I was struggling, how could I think my way out of something or dream bigger when all my mind was doing was telling me how I'd screwed up this far? My ego, or little voice, as Blair Singer calls it, was having a party squashing my efforts to shift, and beating me up.

Then I heard a voice asking me the questions below. I've heard this message for, sadly, at least 10 years on and off, yet I never listened before. Here I was again against a wall, frustrated and feeling like I was spinning my wheels.

One day, I was bouncing on my Cellerciser (a mini-trampoline) and leapt off quickly to get something on the stove, landed on my shoe and rolled my foot, nearly breaking my toe. It turned black and hurt so much. My choices were to laugh or cry. I laughed. What a ridiculous thing to do to myself! Clearly there was a message I wasn't paying attention to.

A new girl had come into my life and asked me, "Have you received a message you are listening to?" "NO!" I said emphatically. She pressed on, "Are you sure, not even something small?" Again I said, "NO, No... okay well there is this one thing but it's totally insignificant." "What is it?" she asked.

Who is God? God is whoever you believe him to be. We all come from our own perspective. We have been raised in different religions with different beliefs. This experiment supports them all. You may believe in God, Allah, Buddha, Latzu, universal or cosmic consciousness, or mother nature... all of them are welcomed and okay. God is my choice and what I believe in.

My main belief is God always wants us to be the best version of ourselves. If we are created in the likeness and image of God, then we too have the ability to be the designers of our lives. I adopt a philosophy that gives us the ability to create the life we desire.

Yet, the focus of this experiment is not to create our own life. Rather it is to see what God would do with our lives if we just gave him the opportunity. What is his vision for you? What does he believe to be true about you? What would your life be like 30 days from now if you just trusted his vision and beliefs?

This is about living the highest vision of yourself and having a personal cheerleader guiding you along the way.

How this came to be:

I was struggling in my life, still picking up the pieces after getting out of an abusive marriage. I'd return to a pattern or rather find myself again in a familiar place and couldn't seem to find my way out. I felt ashamed that I was repeating the same lesson over again and my results hadn't shifted much since the last time I was here.

I was struggling financially, I'd lost my passion in my career, getting stuck in my skill rather than my gifts. I wasn't fulfilled and was in the process of switching my career into something that got me inspired again to help people and make a difference.

Introduction

Welcome to "Experiment with God" (EWG). I'm so thrilled you are joining me on this journey. The mission of EWG is to live God's vision and what he believes to be true about you for the next 30 days.

I was going through a challenging time that seemed to last exceptionally long. Have you ever felt that way? I kept praying and asking for a solution. The only thing that came to me was this voice in my head saying to me, "What if you believe what I believe to be true about you for 30 days? What if you live my vision of your life as if it's true for 30 days? My response was, "Do you have anything else?" Sad, but true. It wasn't until I nearly broke my toe and was laid up, unable to work, that I finally took action on these questions.

I thought, what's the worst that could happen? The worst-case scenario is I'll be in the exact same spot, feeling the same amount of stress. Then it occurred to me, what if it worked? It's only an experiment and it's only 30 days. Honestly, I have nothing to lose except maybe a little time.

Before we dive into this process, I'm not here to tell you who GOD is or who GOD should be to you. This is first and foremost an individual process. We all have our own beliefs and faith, and that is great! All I ask is that you bring your version of GOD to the table, provided that GOD is someone or something to you that only thinks highly of you and only sees the best in you.

There is no NEGATIVE talk from GOD. That isn't GOD anyway. This is not about your inner critic speaking up or expressing another disappointed voice.

going for you, more than you know, and such an opportunity ahead. There is so much more waiting for you. I believe in you. Trust the process, show up and see what happens.

In faith,

Christiana

To Freddie Agnir, having you come into my life has shifted it for the better. It wasn't until you, that I've had someone I could truly rely on. You are such an incredible partner and my biggest champion. I am so proud to be with you. You are an incredible man. Thank you for taking such great care doing the first round of edits and writing such an incredible poem that encompasses what this journey is all about. You've given me the courage to step up and shine brighter. I hope everyone gets to know the blessing of having a relationship like ours. You are my rock, my anchor in rough times, and my inspiration to keep reaching higher in life. Thank you for being my best friend and partner.

To Brené Brown, it's your work on vulnerability and shame that I have been leaning on, especially with putting this message out into the world. My favorite speech of yours that I watch quite often is "It's Not the Critic Who Counts..." from 99 Design. Thank you for your bravery and vulnerability to show up and share. You've paved the way for me and so many others. I can't express how grateful I am to keep learning from you.

To Andrew Brooke, my book architect, and Lisa Browning, my editor, thank you for working with me to bring this book to life. I am so grateful for your care, consideration and quick responses to achieve my deadlines. Thank you!

There are so many more people to thank. My apologies if I've left anyone out. I believe every person that's entered my life along the way has had an impact on me to make me who I am today. I am grateful for each of you and every experience. It's because of those experiences the good, the challenging and the wonderful that I'm here now. You've touched my life and made it richer. Thank you.

To those who are reading this book, it's for you that I am putting this out there. Thank you for taking the time to read this book and experience it for yourself. I am so grateful for the opportunity to share this message. You are the reason I am doing this. You have so much to embrace this process and bring it to life. Thanks for being such an incredible friend and inspiration. Shawn Gibson, C.J., Linda Perkins, David Thunder, Genevieve Coleman, Sean Adams, Lynn Beasley, Jessica Dean, Mary Glorfield, Darren LaCroix, Dilys Murphy, Jamie Beavers, Navi Rawat and Dan Safkow, each of you have been there for me and inspired me to stay on the path and keep going. I am so grateful to have you in my life. You mean the world to me. Thank you for being there.

To my coach, Mimi Peak, thank you for seeing the best in me and guiding me with such care. You keep me on track, and since we've been working together, everything is falling into place. I am so grateful for your time, energy and counsel.

To my mentors, Alex Mandossian, Clinton Swaine, T. Harv Eker, and Blair Singer, you've pushed me to grow and show up in a bigger way. You've all made such an impact on my life. I'm grateful for your time, energy and counsel.

To Raymond Aaron, thank you for encouraging me to publish this book. I had been sitting on it and keeping it quiet. It was your enthusiasm for this idea and what is possible from it that got me off the bench to finish it. Thanks for believing in me and pushing me to take action.

To Neale Donald Walsch, your book *Conversations with God* was such a big turning point for me. You let me know the voice I heard was God, and that opened our dialogue even further. I bought *CWG Book 1* for my father when he was dying of cancer in 1997, and because of your courage to put that book out, my father had his first direct experience of God! He had such peace in the end, having that personal relationship with God. Words can't express how much that means and what you've done. It's shaped my life in a very big way. I am most grateful for you. It's given me the courage to put *Experiment with God* out into the world. Thank you.

Acknowledgments

First, I want to thank you, God, for being so patient. I didn't listen for such a long time. You've stuck by me and have been so supportive of me even though I was resisting this process and procrastinating bringing this out into the world. You've always been beside me and encouraging me. I am incredibly grateful for our relationship and your support.

Second, my parents have been my champions. My father was always pushing me to go for my dreams and live my best life. He introduced me to personal development and always believed in me. My mother is my cheerleader. She is the kindest person I know. She always has something nice to say and offers words of encouragement. Even when I was scared to get this message out, she kept cheering me on. My Aunt Lucy and Uncle Norm, you've always been consistent in supporting me even though you didn't understand my choices. Thank you.

To my closest friends, you've stood by me even when things were bleak and inspired me to keep going. Marjean Holden, you've been my best friend and helped me when I needed it most. Thank you for all those nights, conversations and processing. Most of all our incredible belly laughs. I am so grateful for you. Thank you for being there for me. Miriam Serman, you've helped me through some of the roughest times and helped me process the pain and healing. Words can't express my deepest gratitude. Thank you. Karen Albert, you are such a good friend. Thanks for always being there to brighten my mood, talk in accents and make me laugh. You've been a cheerleader to get this message out. Thank you for that. Anthony Lee, watching you go after your dreams and bring your vision to life has inspired me

Foreword

I first met Christiana Carter when she was the Assistant Trainer at New Peaks, a personal development training company, when I was speaking at their event. She was able to raise the energy of the room beyond anyone I've seen before. I noticed her innate ability to connect with the audience, capture their attention and get them genuinely excited about new possibilities and she will be able to captivate you. So, when she told me about *Experiment with God,* I immediately saw the connection between this innovative, insightful work and how Christiana engages with those around her.

I am extremely impressed with Christiana's process in *Experiment with God.* It's not every day a book comes along that surprises me. I've been publishing for quite some time now, so when Christiana shared this idea with me, I knew I wanted to publish her Experiment.

After reading this powerful book, I recommend it as a must read! What makes this book so fascinating is that it offers a simple process to help you discover the still, small voice inside yourself, and develop your own unique communication with God. What an extraordinary experience!

Take a journey by reading this book and discovering the experiment for yourself. There is no way to do it wrong. This book contains a simple, easy strategy to develop your own relationship with God. You'll be so glad you did!

I highly recommend Christiana and *Experiment with God*!

Raymond Aaron
New York Times Best Selling Author

Contents

Let me ask you, are you more grateful for your health before or after you've been sick?

Taking stock removes the conversation of your little voice. It's simple to picture the things that make my heart open or light up, and things that touch me in a deeper way. It's much easier for me to connect to those things and develop my appreciation in this way.

Step 2: Belief System
What would God believe to be true if he was living your life?

This seemed easier for me when I was thinking what I would believe to be true if I believed what God believed about me. How would I act, what would I think, what would my initial thoughts be?

Again, many thought leaders will tell us to adopt a more positive belief system, yet in my experience there was always resistance, and that voice inside my head saying, "This isn't you; you are faking it." This voice would just berate me and be so cruel.

However, when it was what God believed to be true, it took me out of the equation because I was adopting someone else's version of truth. My little voice had nothing to object to; it wasn't my beliefs to attack. This is only an experiment so I get to play with these for 30 days to see if my life changes for the better.

Step 3: What is God's Vision for my life?
What does he believe to be true about me? What does he say to me? What's possible from his perspective for my life and who I can become?

Once again, initially I was adopting the idea of writing the script for my life. Yet I found that I didn't reach as high because if I wrote it down, then I was responsible for making it happen and my ego kept looking for ways I wasn't succeeding.

However, if I'm listening to what God thinks my vision is or what's possible for me, then the vision is so much greater than what I would come up with for myself. Also it alleviates the pressure of having to fulfill the vision. Instead I get to show up, experiment, and see what happens if I choose to believe what he believes about me.

This slight shift in perspective takes away the work and instead fills me with a sense of wonder of what's possible doing this experiment. I'm excited each day to show up and see what he has to say. It's fun to sit down, get in this mindset, and see what shows up. I'm just along for the ride. Fulfilling my end of the bargain is just committing daily to the writing and reading; the how is out of my control and I'm fully okay with it.

After all, if it doesn't work, I haven't lost anything. I've lived the past 30 days believing and thinking better things than I have ever thought about myself consistently. It's a win/win experiment.

If God is telling me his vision of my life, then anything is possible. It doesn't have to happen, just be the possibility I could live into. This is the distinction that makes this work. What if he could be right?

Have you ever had that experience of someone believing in you? I did, and what I realized is I would fight harder to be the person they thought I was. What is it about living into another's vision of us that causes us to act bigger than for ourselves?

We see this in families. If you tell kids how ugly or unworthy they are, they will live into that reality. However, if you consistently tell them what's possible, how amazing they are and list out their best qualities, you'll find they start living into that vision you have of them.

The same is true with this process. I got so excited to see what God's vision of my life is that by day 6 it turned into a dialogue as I found resistance in myself. Now when we communicate, I find whatever challenges come up, he will speak into those challenges and offer wisdom on what's possible from there.

WAYS TO IMPLEMENT THIS EXPERIMENT:

1: Follow along day by day in the book.
My mother at age 75 started this process and had trouble hearing the still small voice inside. To help anyone that may be in a similar situation, I've added the practice to the end of each day in the book so you can follow along.

Either write your own steps or use what speaks to you from what I wrote. There is no wrong way to do this process.

It's more important to get started and open the lines of communication.

2: Dive in and create your own journal separate from the book.
There is no need to follow along with the book. I am putting my journal out there for those who would like more support. This could be on computer or hand written journal. Choose what works best for you.

3: Use it as healing.
Maybe you have a strong opinion of God, avoid God or hate God.
If things are rough right now or your faith is lacking, THAT's okay.

One woman who did this process started out with writing hate letters to God. If you have that experience, you aren't wrong, you just need to vent and heal. All is welcome.

We only ask that you only re-read the positive feedback.

If you feel like venting letters or frustration letters are in order, simply record those separately from this process. Until the shift, then re-read the positive responses only.

Christiana Carter

Do your best to complete Taking Stock and God's Belief System, then write your venting letters in a separate space. Give yourself time and your experience will shift.

In your case, re-read Taking Stock and God's Belief System... then after the quality of your communication becomes positive and supportive, record those in the same space as Step 1&2. Use that as your script to build upon.

Imagine if you adopted this experiment for yourself. What could be possible?

It was the first time I gave myself space from that critical little voice, to let a bigger vision come through without working against it.

What do you think God could do for you and through you in 30 days? He works miracles, and he can work miracles for you too. Discover that still small voice of God within you and let him work through.

Don't take my word for it, do the experiment for yourself. Show up and see what happens. Worst case scenario is you are exactly where you are right now. What's possible? Anything.

In Faith,

Christiana

xxii

Invitation to the Willow

For Christiana
By Freddie Agnir

Stand with me, oh Willow
The earth, while you're at rest
Grounded in simplicity
While drawing out the best

Dance with me, oh Willow
Flutter with my breeze
Harmonize your tender boughs
Entwining as you please

Play with me, oh Willow
The sun's eternity
Awaken what's inside of you
To always be with me

Grow with me, oh Willow
Like water for the soul
A partnership upon my stage
Accomplishing our goal

Love with me, oh Willow
Your heart opens the gates
Hear my voice; extend the gift
Abundant life awaits

Experiment with God Journal

Day 1: April 11, 2011

Taking Stock: These are moments that take my breath away or make me pause in appreciation, either past or present.

- Horses, horseback riding
- Acting in a play
- Working with my hands
- Woodworking with dad
- Speech class
- Tennis
- Cheerleading (the beginning)
- Gymnastics
- Dancing
- Outrigger canoe racing
- Qi gong
- Meditating (Pranic Healing)
- Volunteer work
- Causes

God's Belief System: If God were living my life, what would he believe to be true?

- The world is conspiring for my highest good.
- I am amazing, and my light lifts others up.
- I am strong, confident and beautiful.
- Every day is an opportunity to make the world a better place.
- I believe that I deserve the very best in life.
- My heart is my greatest asset. How I love people is my healing and theirs.
- I am fearless.
- I am a gift.
- I have a compassionate heart... a true love of helping others.
- My gift is showing others what's possible with their lives.

- I make other people's lives easier for having known me.
- I take the right action every day and moment to moment.
- My light shines brightly to illuminate the path for others to follow.
- I am a generous, kind, loving, compassionate leader.
- I am beautiful.
- I deserve to be well taken care of.
- I love my life and can't wait to jump out of bed and live it.

God's Vision or Message: Get still and listen for the voice or message. What is coming through?

You were created to be the example of me in the world. You are my greatest gift. You are confident, smart, fun, and sexy. You take great care in honoring your body temple. You are full of energy with great enthusiasm for life. People are naturally drawn to you and want to be around you. You use this ability to make a larger impact.

You are special. There is not one person out there like you. You have a unique gift to share with the world. I choose you because you are strong enough to get the message out to help others.

You will transform the world with laughter, joy, and enthusiasm. You reach people and touch them in an intimate way, creating a bond and trust to help them believe in their highest good as well.

People can hear you and your message. Shout it loudly from the rooftops, and get excited to make a difference.

You are known for transforming the world with games and showing people what truly makes a difference.

I have already given you everything you need for success.

There is nothing more you need to learn. Just communicate with me and keep the lines of communication open.

I see you as the best person to unite the world with laughter. Show people that it's not what happens to us that determines our outlook, but rather it is who we want to ultimately be that determines who and what we become. I have so much planned for you, so much more than you can see. Your job is to simply walk each day in faith, knowing that I am providing for you before you even ask. Understand that abundance is the only thing I know. Thoughts of lacking anything is just you feeling disconnected, which isn't possible.

You are loved, valued and adored. You are special and perfect in this moment, just as you are.

Trust my vision for you.

Day 1 Exercise

Taking Stock:
What are 3 things/moments that take your breath away or have you pause with appreciation?

1._____
2._____
3._____

God's Belief System:
What are 3 things God would believe to be true about you?
Or you can use what he said for me?

1._____
2._____
3._____

What is God's vision or message for you?
Get still and listen for the voice or message. What is coming through?
Or what passage from my entry spoke to you?

Experiment with God

Day 2: April 12, 2011

Taking Stock:

- Pranic Healing
- Meditating
- Qi gong
- Dancing
- Workshops/Seminars
- Singing in choir
- Playing beach volleyball
- Traveling
- Canoeing
- Skydiving
- Working with horses
- Sitting outside watching the world go by
- Hanging out with Lucy watching for squirrels
- Teaching
- Helping others through emotional clearings
- Music, especially the cello, makes my heart sing.

God's Belief System:

- I believe the world is conspiring for my greatest good.
- I am exactly perfect in this moment.
- Before I ask, my prayers are answered.
- I am blessed.
- I can do anything.
- I have the power to heal others and myself.
- I am fun, sexy, smart, and it's safe to be me.
- I am a gift, and others' lives are better for knowing me.
- I am compassionate and care deeply for others.
- I am worthy of having all my desires come to pass.
- Being created in the image of God, all the power I need is already within me.

- I am psychic.
- People are inherently good and wish me the best.
- People go out of their way to help me succeed.
- I'm an excellent teacher and trainer.
- My laugh is infectious, and it is my gift to share.
- I am worthy of all the abundance the world can offer.
- I manage my money well and use it to help others.
- Thought leaders are my peer group.
- Laughter is the true power we are all searching for.

God's Vision or Message:

I know you feel disconnected. That isn't possible. I am everywhere and everything, all at once.

You have the most beautiful heart. You care deeply for the smallest of creatures. You have an innocence that has never left. You are compassionate, loyal, and lovable. Yes, lovable! You bring a smile to people's faces without even trying. You are wise beyond your years. You are a giver, but you need to receive the bounty I have waiting for you.

You are a natural beauty. You take excellent care of your body temple. You eat well, exercise regularly and sleep 7 hours every night.

You are a fearless woman, even though you don't always think so. I'm so impressed with who you are turning out to be.

It is safe to rely on others and on me. It's okay to trust me to give you everything you need. You are protected, loved and cared for. You have a vision that the world needs right now. You are safe. You... are... safe.

This is the deal... you have to believe in what I believe to be true about you. You are remarkable, brave and funny. You have such passion for life. It's time to stand up and shine your light. People are waiting for you, and you are committed. You are so very successful, and more success is on its way.

You are a rare and special gift. You are a reflection of me and all that's possible in the world. If you just believe my version of your life and let me work through out, look out world!

It is safe to be successful, beautiful, confident, and connected. At no point have you ever been separate from me; only your mind makes that idea so. Trust your inner guidance...my voice speaking to you.

You are spectacular. I am so grateful for you.

Rest and remember me. You can rest in me always. I have so much energy to give; there is no draining of energy in my presence. Stop searching and start knowing that this is exactly who you are meant to be. Even though others come and go, you must hold true to your purpose and your mission.

Day 2 Exercise

Taking Stock:
What are 3 things/moments that take your breath away or have you pause with appreciation?

1._____
2._____
3._____

God's Belief System:
What are 3 things God would believe to be true about you?
Or you can use what he said for me?

1._____
2._____
3._____

What is God's vision or message for you?
Get still and listen for the voice or message. What is coming through?
Or what passage from my entry spoke to you?

_____
_____
_____
_____
_____
_____
_____
_____
_____
_____
_____
_____

Day 3: April 13, 2011

Taking Stock:

- A sunset
- Sitting or walking on the beach
- Dolphins... always dolphins
- Falling in love
- Meeting someone I've never met, but I remember them and know them
- Watching animals playing
- Watching children play and laugh
- Improv
- Knitting
- Organizing group events
- Game nights with friends or family
- Rocking on a boat, floating on water
- Sailing
- A cool breeze on a hot humid day
- The smell of fall
- When the leaves start turning colors
- The smell of bacon cooking (even though I don't eat it)
- The sound of Wide World of Sports (reminds me of my dad)
- Strawberry Hot Springs
- Conversations with C.J.
- Teaching from stage
- Teaching in general – the moment the other person has their Aha – amazing!
- Grooming a horse
- Sitting underneath a tree
- Climbing the tree
- My first 5-figure month (a very good month indeed)
- Singing in the choir
- Pole dancing (S Factor)
- On stage working with Clinton Swaine

- Knowing my mom is always there just a phone call away
- Marjean, Miriam – the two women I trust with my life.
- My new friends
- When I'm connected to God
- Stillness
- Quiet mind

God's Belief System:

- I am a powerful creator.
- I am unique, and the world is conspiring for my greatest good.
- People come out of the woodwork to help me.
- I am lovable.
- The world is a place where we get to choose who and how we want to be.
- There is so much abundance in the world; just look at the blades of grass or leaves on a single tree.
- Things come to me quickly; I manifest easily and powerfully.
- I deserve all the good the world has to offer.
- I manage my money well and use it not only for myself, but to help others, too.
- I teach, train, love, learn and grow day by day. Everything is for my learning and evolution.
- I trust my inner guidance above all else.
- To have what I want, it is important to stand out from the crowd.
- I'm worthy, lovable and such a gift to the world.
- I am a loyal, true friend.
- Anything to which I apply myself becomes wildly successful.
- I am a charismatic, dynamic, powerful leader
- I see opportunities everywhere.
- Everything I need is provided, even before I ask.
- God takes care of the "how."

God's Vision or Message:

You are so beautiful. I see you are listening to me now and starting to take action. Now, take action every day.

You are a powerful light in this world, and the world needs you to stand up and shine that light.

Trust the messages that come to you. You are only out of practice. Each day, simply walk more in alignment.

You are growing into the person you've wanted to become. You are already there. Just sit back and pay attention.

It's safe to stand up now; the path is clear. It's simple to keep moving from a place of stillness. You'll understand, just sit with it for a while.

We've already created the possibilities for your life. You must however come and get them. It requires you to take a risk. It's all right here. Just start asking for what you need and act when it is given.

I know what you are capable of, and I have big plans for you. You are meant to play a much bigger game. Believe as I do that you can have anything you want. You already do.

You have a strong connection with me. We have always been connected this way. Come back to stillness to hear my voice.

You take great care of your body temple, and are a fit, lean, natural beauty. You are a wonderful, powerful woman. You are so beautiful and lovable. Trust that there is a match for you out there. I'm working on it. Your job is to leave it alone and stay in alignment with me. You are always protected.

You have such a big heart. You care for others deeply. When you walk into a room, it naturally lights up. You bring joy, light and laughter wherever you go. People feel you before they see you. Your energy is powerful and present.

You are strong enough to go after your dreams, and you have a unique ability to put others at ease. People feel comfortable around you. You inspire them to reach their highest potential.

Stop thinking. Write from what you hear me saying.

I love you. No matter what you do, I will not stop loving you. There is nothing you need to become better. Just take action. Simple enough.

You are amazing at helping others to get productive and to work more efficiently. You have an uncanny ability to step up, get involved and make a difference. And you DO make a difference. You inspire people to be more of themselves just by knowing you. You help people on their paths, and you are compensated well for it.

You are a terrific mother, daughter, friend and family member. Walk in faith knowing that you are remarkable, loyal, kind, and compassionate. You are exactly where you are supposed to be in your life right now. I do NOT make mistakes. Everything that is happening will be used by you and will fuel your next phase.

Follow this guide and you are on the path. Believing my thoughts about you for 30 days is very powerful. Trust and keep moving. I won't let you down.

Everyone is conspiring for your good. On this side, you have a team to help you keep your energy up. They are doing all they can to send you regular messages. There are so many rooting for you to win.

Make that your new mantra: root for someone else to win and see what happens.

Day 3 Exercise

Taking Stock:
What are 3 things/moments that take your breath away or have you pause with appreciation?

1._____
2._____
3._____

God's Belief System:
What are 3 things God would believe to be true about you?
Or you can use what he said for me?

1._____
2._____
3._____

What is God's vision or message for you?
Get still and listen for the voice or message. What is coming through?
Or what passage from my entry spoke to you?

Day 4: April 14, 2011

Taking Stock:

- Sharing a laugh with a stranger or friend
- Someone holding the door for me
- Random acts of kindness
- Watching the branches and leaves of a tree blowing in the wind
- Sitting watching the waves at the beach
- Walking hand and hand
- Making a stranger smile
- Dancing
- Road tripping
- Adventures
- Game night with friends
- Hanging out with Goddess Circle
- Goddess Camp
- Inspiring music
- A really great hug
- Feeling connected
- Kundalini Yoga
- Qi Gong
- Hot springs
- A conversation with a friend who makes me laugh
- To know someone is thinking of me
- Appreciation Circles
- My personal angels who remind me of what's possible for my life
- Loving without reservation
- Trust in myself
- Trust in God
- Sitting at the aqueduct watching the water flow by

God's Belief System:

- The world is conspiring for my greatest good.
- People come out of the woodwork to help me succeed.
- I deserve all the best the world has to offer.
- How I love others is my healing ...and theirs.
- Everyone is ultimately good, deep down.
- We are all the same – just reflections.
- Abundance comes when you believe, not when you see it.
- I am amazing and haven't even tapped my full potential yet.
- My gift is helping others through healing.
- I love my life.
- I have the most amazing, grateful, loyal, appreciative clientele.
- I am an in demand as a speaker and a trainer.
- My passion is helping others to wake up.
- Laughter is the most profound gift we have to share, and it offers us the greatest healing.
- I am connected at all times with God.
- I am so grateful for every day that I have on this planet, in this lifetime.
- I use every day wisely.
- I take great care of my body temple.
- I am ready to step into my possibility.

God's Vision or Message:

I am so proud of you for sticking with this process. The transformation is going to be outstanding. You are beautiful, loving, kind, and compassionate. You treat others with great respect, and it gives them the ability to rise above.

You have the most amazing heart. Your desire to help people is only overshadowed by what an incredible friend you are. You are fiercely loyal and loving. There isn't a greater friend than you. Trust in your intuition for I am speaking to you from there, right now.

Once you dreamt of making a huge difference in the world. It wasn't a dream. You have an amazing life in front of you. Children are a part of your journey.

You are brilliant, funny, and talented. It's what you do that has the opportunity to transform the world. Just trust yourself and know that I am loving you through all of it.

Stay firmly focused on YOUR path and trust your own intuition about what to do. As always, I'm here for questions.

You are going to change the world in a remarkable way. You have the ability to laugh through everything, love through everything.

You are such a great catch; know that your man is on his way.

Your life is meant to be facilitating to others. You have the amazing gift to show people what it is that they want. You will create a whole book about it. You are a vision and a visionary.

Day 4 Exercise

Taking Stock:
What are 3 things/moments that take your breath away or have you pause with appreciation?

1._____
2._____
3._____

God's Belief System:
What are 3 things God would believe to be true about you?
Or you can use what he said for me?

1._____
2._____
3._____

What is God's vision or message for you?
Get still and listen for the voice or message. What is coming through?
Or what passage from my entry spoke to you?

_____
_____
_____
_____
_____
_____
_____
_____
_____
_____
_____
_____

_____
_____
_____
_____
_____
_____
_____
_____
_____
_____
_____
_____
_____
_____
_____
_____
_____
_____
_____
_____
_____
_____
_____
_____
_____
_____
_____
_____
_____
_____
_____
_____

Day 5: April 15, 2011

Taking Stock:

- A warm jacket on a cold day
- Good friends hanging out together
- Sharing a meal with friends
- Dancing
- Giving massages
- Healing others
- Nurturing
- A clear night with a full moon
- Being in the mountains
- Listening to someone sing from spirit
- Laughing
- The love of a dog
- Being connected to God
- Staying committed
- Helping someone in need
- The ocean
- Walking on the beach
- Sitting in nature
- Reiki
- The sound of acoustic guitar
- Knowing someone is thinking of me in a loving way
- A good friend
- God as my friend
- A comet in the sky
- Grooming a horse
- Horseback riding
- Qi Gong
- Dahn Yoga
- Kundalini Yoga
- My father

God's Belief System:

- The world is conspiring for my highest good.
- The right people always come into my life.
- People go out of their way to help me.
- Good is a quality inherent in everyone
- My gift is my interaction with people.
- I'm talented, smart, funny, and gorgeous.
- My light makes it okay for others to shine their light.
- Opportunity is everywhere.
- Everything is helping me get to where I want to go.
- I trust the flow and expansion processes.
- I'm an amazing friend, confidante, lover and leader.
- I have the best friends anyone could hope for.
- Clients seek me out to work with me. They are fantastic and love my work.
- It is safe to stand up and speak out.

God's Vision or Message:

I'm so honored that you are staying committed to this process. It's crazy how easily you make friends and talk to strangers. I'm thrilled that you love helping people, no matter what. That will be rewarded.

I know you'll transform many lives during your life. You have no idea how many people you are helping in the process. Trust that I am here for you always.

I know your heart. You are strong, confident, beautiful, and amazing. I know that you are set up for success.

Your mission here is to change every person you run into with a new possibility. You have the ability to put people immediately at ease. You shine brightly and so far have stuck it out. You are building momentum.

It's okay to be tired and to fall asleep. Just finish when you wake up. I love you!

You are connected. You take the time to listen and take action on what I'm saying. You are remarkable. Trust in me. You are my vision for the world, unfolding. Don't block your listening to me by making it more than it is. What will happen, will happen. These are for you, but you are also my bridge to others. I know you are excited. Just wait. You haven't seen anything yet. Remember, every person you meet, that's another opportunity to express the love you feel from me. It's another reflection of a spark that has yet to be fully realized.

You've always known there is something deeper going on here. You are now coming into yourself in a way that you can begin to take action and to share this with others. Your dilemma is that you are thinking about what is happening. This is simply my vision for what's possible in your life and my opportunity to remind you of how incredible you truly are.

Your heart moves me: the way you share yourself with others, your loyalty, and your desire to make a difference. This practice we are beginning isn't so much about what we are doing on the surface. This is more like the opportunity for you to make a pit stop and get filled up again. This moment is your way to heal yourself and reconnect. It's the discipline to trust the message you are receiving, and even if it feels weird, write it down anyway.

This is our time and your time to make a difference. It's not about massive differences at first; start with fine-tuning of your listening. That will naturally reflect and radiate to others around you. I know your heart, your cares, and your concerns. You are special. You are my favorite. Yes, I am able to feel that way about each of you simultaneously.

This listening you are developing is only going to get stronger the more you commit to it and practice. The messages will change from day to day. Sometimes you need to hear who you can be in the world. Other times, I'll address what's going on in your heart. I know what you want. Your prayers are answered. Yes, they are. You love this connection, but where we are going together, you must be able to flow moment by moment without being attached to any ideas about how it unfolds. I feel it when you get attached. You fall out of connection with me. My connection never ceases; you just cease to hear. It's a pattern of your ego doing its job.

When you feel that resistance, stop for a moment and sit with me. I'll tell you what's going on and share with you from there.

You all want what you want, the moment you want it. Is that a true wanting? Who knows for sure? Usually in hindsight, my point of view becomes clearer to you. We are cultivating moving from a place of trust while things unfold, even when you get the feeling that you can't see the whole picture.

You'll pause, check in and trust to keep going or adjust. It's all a winding journey. Each step, though it feels out of sync or like a detour, is serving your deeper understanding, if you'll absorb the lesson.

Why do I resist so much?

You resist because you are conditioned to always be in struggle and you, as a human being, are addicted to drama. That's why it's critical to step aside when you are in conversations that flow that way. Just step back, in those moments, feel into your spirit... into your heart. Does this feel open and uplifting? If not, shift the conversation back to where you would like it to go or simply remove yourself from the situation. If that's not possible, just focus on your breath and breathing in the light. *Light always transmutes the dark around you. Practice this discipline. It's okay to make mistakes or stumble as you are learning. Just keep picking yourself back up, open your heart and go again.*

Let your heart lead you in everything you do. It knows what is going on. It will always lead you where you need to be. When talking with others, feel into your heart. Are they connecting with you? Are they open? So many are sleeping and it's frustrating. I get that. But know that it's only a matter of time before others join you, if you hold your own heart open.

Yes, I hear your fear and your protecting of your energy. Yes, many talk about how to avert or guard against other energies. When you are walking in the space of connection with me and keeping your pipeline open, there is no room for anything you consider negative to manifest. It's when you doubt, second guess yourself or hand over your power you make space for that to show up. You have done that quite a bit.

Here's the thing: I will send you a guide, but you are the guide. This practice right here ...this moment-by-moment connecting. You are now being brave writing what you are hearing without filtering it too much. You are learning to trust in me. I know it sounds like bits and pieces of everything you've ever heard. The message hasn't shifted much. It's simple really. Just stay connected and move from your heart. Don't get derailed by your own wanting when it's strong – check to see if it's coming from a feeling of lacking something.

You are special; you are one of a kind, most certainly. All of you are. Stop striving to be like others and to fit a mold not made for you. This is another of your gifts: this dialogue. You are gaining trust in me every time you stop and listen to me.

For now, just sit and pay attention to your thoughts coming and going while staying focused on deep breathing. Practice that for a while and do it anywhere, anytime. There is no perfect place, just as there is no perfect time to connect with me or no perfect medium. It shifts as necessary.

Yes, feel the love. That is me giving you love, reminding you how special you are. I see you and I always have. You are a strong, confident woman. I'll keep reminding you. You risk yourself in connecting with others. You've shifted so much of yourself, yet your core never shifts. You believe in me; you believe in others.

Release those you are holding in a small space, you are constricting your own development by keeping them small. We all get messy on this path. No one is immune. Be compassionate and uphold others to the vision of who they are becoming. You are all running the same direction. Help each other with the momentum. Some may need to stop and rest; some might look like they are going on a detour. Send them love anyway. Be compassionate anyway. There is always someone in front of or behind you in line. Yet there is no in front of or behind, or a line for that matter. Yet the example is needed to explain. The mission is the same to express through you in the physical form.

Yes, this has grown from a simple vision of your life into a dialogue. Keep going anyway. You are loved, valued, adored, part of me, and a reflection of me. Play in your life. Play big. Expand your thinking to see what's possible. I will continue to show you. Foster that vision in others. What's possible for your life? What's possible for today? Who do you want to meet today?

Day 5 Exercise

Taking Stock:
What are 3 things/moments that take your breath away or have you
pause with appreciation?

1._____
2._____
3._____

God's Belief System:
What are 3 things God would believe to be true about you?
Or you can use what he said for me?

1._____
2._____
3._____

What is God's vision or message for you?
Get still and listen for the voice or message. What is coming through?
Or what passage from my entry spoke to you?

_____
_____
_____
_____
_____
_____
_____
_____
_____
_____
_____

Day 6: April 16, 2011

Taking Stock:

- A baby smiling
- A comfy bed
- That first morning stretch as I roll over before fully waking
- Sitting in the sun and feeling the warmth
- Snow balls
- A smile from a stranger
- That feeling of love in my heart, right now
- Falling in love
- That feeling of being in love/appreciation with everyone
- Appreciation circles
- A cup of tea
- A roaring fire
- Rocking on the ocean in a boat
- Watching the fish swim in a lake
- Kayaking
- Playing games with friends
- Music
- A massage
- An open heart
- Icicles on trees
- A full moon
- Kindness of a stranger
- Bumping into an old friend or acquaintance
- A hot shower

God's Belief System:

- The world is conspiring for my greatest good.
- People are coming out of the woodwork to help me.
- I have the most amazing friends in the world.
- I love my life.

- I am blessed every moment of every day.
- Manifesting is effortless.
- I manage my finances with ease.
- Money flows to me easily.
- My heart and how I love is healing and is a gift.
- People are inherently good.
- I am fit, lean and take excellent care of my body temple.
- Laughter is the healing for the planet.

God's Vision or Message:

You are remarkable. There are much bigger plans going on for you. I've got lots of great things lined up for your future. My vision for you is to touch others' hearts. You have an uncanny ability to open people up and give them incentive to make necessary shifts in their lives. You are more than what you are doing now. We haven't even scratched the surface of where you are headed.

This is your moment, your moment to shine. You have an uncanny ability to apply learning in such a way as to make a sizable difference.

I know you are saying your mind is tired. It's just your mind fighting against what is inevitable. Your mind doesn't want you to wake up to what's possible for your life, so it will play as fatigued. Know that I understand what's happening. Your mind's job is to keep you playing small. This process is actually rewiring your brain.

People open their hearts to you. You witnessed that first-hand today. They welcome you in to make a sizable difference.

Now that you are talking about a book, you want to sound like you are put together. You aren't, so stop faking it. You are only getting interesting. Here's the insight: this is only going to work if this remains unedited.

When you were out today watching others, you took a table of 3 people and just with this concept got them turned on to their lives. Imagine the ripple that can come out of this process.

Day 6 Exercise

Taking Stock:
What are 3 things/moments that take your breath away or have you pause with appreciation?

1._____
2._____
3._____

God's Belief System:
What are 3 things God would believe to be true about you?
Or you can use what he said for me?

1._____
2._____
3._____

What is God's vision or message for you?
Get still and listen for the voice or message. What is coming through?
Or what passage from my entry spoke to you?

Day 7: April 17, 2011

Taking Stock:

- Good friends
- Travel
- Adventure
- Meeting like-minded people
- Instant connection
- Love
- Being in love
- Falling in love
- Cheering someone on to be their best
- Birds chirping
- The squishy sound humming birds make when they sing
- Sitting in front of a crackling fire
- The feel of grass under my bare feet
- Cartwheels
- Laying in the grass soaking in the sun
- Connecting with another human being
- The feel of the wind in my hair
- A hug
- A smile
- Faith in myself
- Faith in God
- Kindness of a stranger
- Laughter, always laughter
- Road trips
- Being a light for others
- Speaking truth for others

God's Belief System:

- The world is conspiring for my greatest good.
- I am amazing, wonderful, and beautiful.

- I trust myself and God.
- I know that everything that happens is serving me in some way.
- There is only good to be recognized and appreciated in others.
- I focus on what I want to expand.
- I create amazing teams around me to facilitate my visions.
- My laughter is my healing for the world.
- We are so incredible and just need to be reminded.
- I love myself fully exactly as I am.
- I am fit, lean and healthy, and take great care of my body temple.
- I love without regard or holding back.
- I have this ability to get others to open up.
- I use this ability to help them achieve their highest potential.
- I am always connected, in every moment.
- Everything I want is delivered even before I ask.
- People are coming out of the woodwork to help me excel.
- I wake people up to their greatest potential.
- I love with my whole being.
- I have the best friends and associates around me.
- I surround myself with people who are committed to making a positive difference on the planet.
- I am blessed.
- I am worthy, valued and loved.
- Everything that happens serves me and fosters my growth.
- People always bring out their best when they are around me.
- I create heart connections with people.
- I am grateful every day for everything in my life.

God's Vision or Message:

You are such a beautiful spirit. You have such a desire to help people. The key to all of this is first helping you. This is the incubation period for which we discover one another and grow together. We strengthen our relationship and my vision for your life. You are just a baby in this field, which is exactly where I want you to be. You are willing to serve others, so willing to give and give and give. Hear me now. There is no rush. There is much for you to do, many lives for you to touch. You can be as big or as little as you want. My vision is of you transforming the world. Now, I know that on a deeper level that scares you, and that your ego is certain to keeping butting in. That too is all part of the process.

Here's the deal:

You have this ability to lead with your heart and to open people up. You have such a love of life to share; you are passionate and care deeply for others. More often than not, you put them first. In order for you to step into the vision I have for you, our time together is going to grow you, to strengthen you, have you make time to put yourself first, and to develop the discipline and truth of your own heart. From there, anything is possible.

I know now that you've seen the vision of this little experiment you thought was harmless and invaluable on a large scale, but now you see its potential. Don't worry about what hasn't yet arrived. It's always about staying firmly placed in your center.

You are developing a rhythm of life with me. You have to believe what I believe.

You are smart, funny, sexy, beautiful, grateful, loving, kind, innocent, full of hope, and love to be of service. That's just the beginning. You are compassionate, sweet, tender, open, trustworthy, loyal and, most of all, sincere. You trust me to step into this vision of you. Do you even realize the amazing impact you have on those around you? Just look at lunchtime yesterday, your little experiment of sharing this work. See what happened? Look at how quickly you not only connected, but created a community. This is how we are going to bring the world together. Building this awareness and community, with you so willing to risk your love, heart and self, how can people not fall in love with you and want to be a part of it. We aren't going for total inclusion. First we are looking for those looking for us. Then as we grow together, it will spread. And the ripple effect will create its own momentum.

You aren't responsible for the wisdom; just pass on the wisdom. Yes, you have concerns, but you'll do it anyway because in your heart, it's about opening. I love what Jennifer said yesterday, "You are an orchestrator of the heart, creating heart symphonies wherever you go." That is just the icing on the cake.

You have such a gift of helping others to become the best version of themselves. You do this with such grace and compassion, and most of all, without judgment. I'm so proud of you. Laughter just follows you around. Not that you need to be funny, but your love of life radiates from you. You naturally lighten every room into which you walk.

Now is the time to prepare for what's ahead. My belief in you is evident, wherever you go. Here's what's happening now: you want to hold onto things, places, and people. I promise you this: every person that is supposed to be in your life will stay there. Not every person is supposed to stay the whole time. Many people pass through your life, some steer you in the right direction or help you adjust your course. You tend to stumble with your attachment to the feeling of safety. You are even attached to what you think this will look like. Right now you are wondering, "How am I going to market this dialogue?"

Just let it go... the illusion of control... and see what happens. It's bigger than you can see and that's where trusting and flowing moment by moment will help you with how things transition from here.

Safety is being here in this instant, with me right now. But this is also misleading. You are and have always been safe. Nothing can truly ever harm you. I'll repeat it: nothing can truly ever harm you.

Keep putting one foot in front of the other and walking beside me. We always have stood side by side. We are the same. There is no one bigger than you or lower than you. The elitism isn't real; it's a game some are playing for the sake of playing and belonging. Look instead for those with light in their eyes and a willingness to open their hearts. They are the ones that will affect awakening. It's not about status or money. It's something that is available to every single being. We are all equipped. Not one person is lacking anything they need to live my vision of them.

Remind them for me as you go. They are all complete, worthy, perfect, and loved. It has always been that way and will always be so.

I love you deeply and stand beside you at all times. Whatever you need, I've already delivered. Just pay attention and stay open!

Breathe when you want to hold on and trust. Grab life with both hands, and let your spirit shine. I love you!

Wow, I just want to stay in communication with you and write down what we have to talk about. I just had the most amazing experience of wisdom coming through me. I'm also frustrated that I can't see where all this is going quite yet. I catch glimpses here and there but overall I don't feel like I have anything tangible to hold onto. Jessica said to me, "Right now all you are doing is defining point A."

That's what this process is about. This connection is where everything will grow or be birthed. You are such a special person. I see how quickly you adopt and implement. This is the main focus for right now. Complete this process. Enroll 10 others into doing this experiment as well. After they have completed the process, you will start to truly see what is unfolding. You'll begin to see the patterns and what's possible. Publish these into a book. Let others be a part of the process. Don't edit what you are receiving. Be brave and write anyway, knowing that you are safe, protected. People will get exactly what they need from this. It's the power of a community of tapped-in people, the power of an awakened group. You are just to deliver the message and let things take on a life of their own. There is a bigger plan working, and you are part of it.

As far as my vision for you with other aspects of your life, you will have more clients than you know what to do with because you are ready to receive. This process is about waking up your ability to receive messages and trust what you get. It's only 30 days. Check it out. The commitment is low. See what happens. You are doing an experiment. If you don't like it, don't continue.

Simple is always the best course of action. Nothing needs to be complicated unless you choose to make it so. I am so proud of you. I hear your mind running circles, wondering how this is all happening and wanting to explain it away as you being you or not trusting the work. It's normal, and your ego is just doing its job. At least it's good at its job. The beauty of you is your faith in me to continue and see what happens. I hope others feel the same. The message is different for each person. Everyone brings himself or herself to the conversation. Their personal filter will initially shape the value of the discussion. I will find my path through their filter, if they just stick with it.

This is exciting for you and exciting for me. I held your hand last night, did you feel me?

Yes, I was weeping. I felt your hand in mine, and before I knew it, I was weeping over the beauty of the music that Richard Marx was playing.

Your heart is opening and things will feel uncomfortable for a while because the feeling is new. That's part of the transition. You are getting yourself ready for the next part. Just trust that you are safe and that this is all part of the plan.

So you want to know what my vision is for you. I see you standing on a platform, teaching this message to people all over the world. It's simple and straightforward.

This message is about people opening their eyes to what's possible, if they live my vision for them. I also see you uniting the world in laughter and games. You have a voice to help others. Your unique ability to open your heart and be vulnerable from stage is the exact combination that will make this successful.

Don't pigeonhole what this could be. It's still much bigger than you think. The organizing is going to transform those skills into a different entity so just be open for shifts in how that unfolds.

Why don't you give me greater specifics for my life?

If I told you what was possible too quickly, you will get stuck in the larger vision before you lay the foundation. I see you working with the thought leaders to help them deliver their messages in ways that people can assimilate the content and

start living it from an experiential place. People learn through experience, not through listening. Touch them in their own minds and let them feel what you are talking about. It's remarkable.

How come I get tired every time we do this?

It's your body's way of taking you out.

You are my favorite person. There is not another like you. You are my favorite version of you. There is so much we still have to share and learn about one another.

Day 7 Exercise

Taking Stock:
What are 3 things/moments that take your breath away or have you pause with appreciation?

1._____
2._____
3._____

God's Belief System:
What are 3 things God would believe to be true about you?
Or you can use what he said for me?

1._____
2._____
3._____

What is God's vision or message for you?
Get still and listen for the voice or message. What is coming through?
Or what passage from my entry spoke to you?

_____
_____
_____
_____
_____
_____
_____
_____
_____
_____
_____

Day 8: April 18, 2011

Taking Stock:

- A rainy day
- Good friends
- Traveling
- A nap
- Making someone's life work easier
- The sound of birds singing
- A bath
- A roaring crackling fire
- Knowing someone loves me

God's Belief System:

- The world is conspiring for my greatest good.
- I meet the nicest people wherever I go.
- People go out of their way to help me.
- I manage my money with ease and excellence.
- Life is inherently good.
- Abundance is everywhere. Just look at the blades of grass.
- My heart opens up other people.
- I love my life.
- I see the best in people.
- I am psychic.
- God is always there for me. We talk all the time.
- Everything is provided even before I ask.
- Every day is a chance to make a difference.
- I radiate joy, love and enthusiasm wherever I go.
- I am blessed.
- I am loved, beautiful, sexy, fun and happy.
- People love me exactly as I am.
- I am loyal, loving, kind and compassionate.
- I care deeply for animals.

- I love being a cheerleader helping others achieve their goals.

God's Vision or Message:

I am so proud of you. Not only are you standing in your power and commitment to this process and me, you are sharing this gift with others and they feel your heart, passion, enthusiasm, and commitment. You are remarkable. It's only getting better. I know sometimes you wonder what will happen in all of this. Remember the premise: this too is still an experiment. You only need to show up daily and do the work. It will take on a life of its own.

You are gorgeous and such a love. You reach out to people with your whole heart. Remember to keep your eye open for the spark of recognition. Start with those people. Not everyone is awake.

I want you to keep up the good work. It's just the beginning. This process is creating for you a platform and foundation from which you'll be able to manifest, create, speak, and share yourself. Remember to have fun and let it all go. Play first and see what happens. I know it's easy to get knocked off, but you've had that experience and used these principles to put yourself right back on target.

You keep looking for brilliance in every communication and feel like you are not living up to your potential if it's not fantastic. Just relax. Take the pressure off yourself, and don't make this about you. You are solely responsible for showing up each day and downloading whatever you hear. Sometimes it will be more insightful than others; sometimes I will be easier to hear than other days; and sometimes your mind will block the channel. The key is to keep at it. Commit to the daily practice, and it will unfold before you.

If you come at this with expectations, it gives me little room to express and expand. I only know expansion. Don't limit me with your thinking. You do that enough for yourself. Come back to the beginning each time and start there. Just wait, listen for something to come through, and then start typing again. Like any relationship, there will be highs and lows. Yet, with me it's constant. It's only your ability and discipline to tap in that has you experience ups and downs. You'll continue to develop through all of this and find your own keel. It's really wonderful to watch you flourish in this process.

There is much to come in the next month. I've got the how worked out, and it will reveal itself. Stay in the enjoyment and see what happens. Play. It's all about what's possible from my vantage point. I have far more than you can imagine.

Will I have a family of my own?

Yes, you will. I will send you the children that need you, and it will work out effortlessly. That isn't now or in the near future. Trust it's coming and leave it to me.

You are smart, funny, and kind. You are a bright light shining the way for others to follow. People are drawn to your brightness. You'll show them the way to their own light by radiating your truth so naturally. This is going to help get people connected with me and to build relationships with me.

Your business is growing rapidly. Remember your worth and don't discount it. What you are able to do for people is a beautiful opportunity to help them on their way. Valuing yourself properly will show others how to value themselves as well.

Sleep well.

Day 8 Exercise

Taking Stock:
What are 3 things/moments that take your breath away or have you pause with appreciation?

1._____
2._____
3._____

God's Belief System:
What are 3 things God would believe to be true about you?
Or you can use what he said for me?

1._____
2._____
3._____

What is God's vision or message for you?
Get still and listen for the voice or message. What is coming through?
Or what passage from my entry spoke to you?

Day 9: April 19, 2011

Taking Stock:

- A cup of tea
- A warm bath
- A massage
- The sound of someone laughing
- Sitting in a ray of sun
- Watching a hawk soar overhead
- A full moon
- Great friends
- Marjean picking me up from the airport late at night
- A really great hug
- Cold water on my face
- Things that make me laugh
- The sound of running water
- This project
- Helping people
- A smile from a stranger
- My favorite music
- Knowing I can help someone
- Staying centered
- Trusting myself
- Following my inner guidance
- Hearing the laughter of my neighbors echo into my room

God's Belief System:

- The world is conspiring for my greatest good.
- I love my life.
- Good things always happen to me.
- I see the best in everyone.
- I am blessed.
- My prayers are answered even before I ask.

- Everything I need is provided.
- Laughter is my greatest gift.
- People feel better being around me.
- People are coming out of the woodwork to help me.
- I am talented, beautiful, and successful. I am a terrific entrepreneur.
- I always see opportunity and possibility.
- I follow through with projects I start.
- I am strong, confident and am self-motivated.
- There is more than enough time to do everything I want.
- I take time to nurture my soul with silence and meditation.
- The connection to God is always open.

God's Vision or Message:

This project is just getting started. Keep on top of getting it going. The right people will be a part of this journey. The plan is so much bigger. There is so much more to come of it.

Don't get distracted in the details. You are focusing down the road instead of just doing the process. Sometimes you can take yourself out with that kind of thinking. You have a remarkable life filled with friends, family and people who naturally support you. Many times, though, you forget to remember how lucky you are.

Good job taking a day of rest to let yourself unwind. I also noticed your resistance to sit down and continue the process. Your lazy brain wanted to take you out of the process saying, "Just skip one day, it won't matter."

The truth is, it DOES matter. Each day is critical in this 30-day process. This is exciting, and again you are developing a pattern, habit and relationship of listening and trusting yourself and me. You are strong and powerful. You'll need that for what we are doing. So many people are going to be waking up, and you are doing this work and getting the others ready to begin their process.

I'm thrilled about your commitment. I know you are risking a lot by putting yourself out there and exposing these letters to the world. By standing, others may choose to lash out. Here is the beauty in all of that: no one can touch you or hurt you. It's just not possible. The only way you are able to be hurt is if you choose to let them and you focus on negativity. If you stay connected with me and trust my vision, it's only going to get better. You don't need to protect your energy or guard yourself in any way.

You are protected, safe and loved. Remember I am always with you, standing beside you. At no point are we ever disconnected. The only ups and downs you experience with us are on your end. I am always constant. You are developing your stamina to stay in this space with me. This process is about cultivating that strength of heart, spirit, mind and soul. You will bond with others and create communities to foster this awareness. Each of you will bring yourself to the equation. This is not about all agreeing in one way or joining some group. This is about gaining back your power to trust your own voice deep within you, the voice that is rooting for you to be the best version of yourself that you can possibly be.

I know your heart. I feel you at all times. I understand your concerns and worries. Have you noticed your worries have been so much less since you started this process? It's exciting isn't it? Just wait!

Sleep well. Get some rest. Tomorrow will be amazing!

Day 9 Exercise

Taking Stock:
What are 3 things/moments that take your breath away or have you pause with appreciation?

1._____
2._____
3._____

God's Belief System:
What are 3 things God would believe to be true about you?
Or you can use what he said for me?

1._____
2._____
3._____

What is God's vision or message for you?
Get still and listen for the voice or message. What is coming through?
Or what passage from my entry spoke to you?

Day 10: April 20, 2011

This day got deleted! So this is your opportunity to practice for yourself.

Day 10 Exercise

Taking Stock:
What are 3 things/moments that take your breath away or have you pause with appreciation?

1._____
2._____
3._____

God's Belief System:
What are 3 things God would believe to be true about you?
Or you can use what he said for me?

1._____
2._____
3._____

What is God's vision or message for you?
Get still and listen for the voice or message. What is coming through?
Or what passage from my entry spoke to you?

_____
_____
_____
_____
_____
_____

Christiana Carter

66

Day 11: April 21, 2011

Taking Stock:

- An ocean view
- A sense of family
- Laughter
- The sound of birds singing
- The ocean
- A kitten
- A puppy
- My car when it's warm from the sun
- A hot shower
- A massage
- A Jacuzzi
- A hot spring
- Falling in love
- The feel of grass between my toes
- Cartwheels
- Running
- Watching a tree blowing in the wind
- Making someone laugh
- Making new friends
- A great kiss
- Holding hands
- A chill in the air
- The first days of autumn
- Snow days
- Quiet
- Moments of presence
- Taking a walk and watching the world go by
- Playing with my dog

God's Belief System:

- The world is conspiring for my good.
- People go out of their way to help me.
- Life is an opportunity to be whatever I choose to be.
- Whatever I need is provided for me before I ask.
- I am loving, kind, fun and beautiful.
- I deserve the very best life has to offer.
- Money flows to me easily.
- My finances are always handled and are growing exponentially.
- Abundance is all around me.
- People are inherently good.
- I meet the coolest, kindest people wherever I go.
- I am protected and loved.
- I am a gift.
- My laugh is healing.
- How I love is healing.
- I trust myself and I trust my connection with God explicitly.
- I have a knowing inner guidance that keeps me on track.
- I am perfect just as I am.
- Everything I need, I already have.
- All the answers lie in stillness.
- I am enough.
- I am worthy of being treated well and being taken care of.

God's Vision or Message:

I know you've been letting fear get the better of you the last two days. The more you see what's coming, the more you are getting nervous. There is nothing to be nervous about. This is my vision for your life, and you are doing fantastic. I know you have a tendency to hide when you get scared.

Remember you are living my vision of your life for 30 days and believing what I believe about you. That means when you come to a place of fear or feel overwhelmed, just go outside and take a moment to reconnect with me. Remember, you are always safe. Keep trusting in me, and I'll take care of you.

I know your heart. You know mine. We are in this together. You keep going. I know you are frustrated that yesterday's entry got deleted. Things happen. It will all work out. Just stay with it. This isn't about being perfect; it's about showing up to see what happens. Have faith that I have a better plan for you. It's your discovery mission. Remember each day to focus on being in harmony with me a little more. When you see my vision for you, start living into it. Trust it. Trust me. I have your back and will not let you down. I know you've been scared to trust. This is your opportunity to step into the possibility that it's okay to trust you and me.

Mistakes are critical to our growth. We don't learn without them. So embrace all perceived mistakes as the truth; they are opportunity to refine what you are doing and choose differently next time.

You are confident, funny, successful, and full of hope for a bright future. You have always wanted to save people. That is part of who you are. This project will give you the opportunity to let others save themselves or give themselves a remarkable gift. Just be compassionate. Remember how long it took you to finally listen to the message. It's about looking in the mirror and taking off the glasses that are skewing your vision from the truth.

You are a gift. And you are so remarkable. You are to continue to speak on behalf of this project and to also trust that this process will be exactly what it needs to be. Your business will thrive, and now you can see the possibility that you are not just here for your physical effort, but rather your mind is the moneymaker and the transformation agent. I'm happy that you are finally seeing into the light of what's possible with your business. It's not going to stay the same; it will transform itself into something else altogether. The parts that serve you best will remain. This has just been your training ground to listen and practice executing the instructions you receive. You are on the right path.

This is the platform that will give you the opportunity to speak on a larger stage. It's coming soon, so get ready. It's okay to have some downtime. Just keep an eye on things. Sometimes you get sucked in, and it mutes my voice. You are remarkable, and I know you will do great. I trust you. I love you. Go speak and inspire.

Day 11 Exercise

Taking Stock:
What are 3 things/moments that take your breath away or have you pause with appreciation?

1._____
2._____
3._____

God's Belief System:
What are 3 things God would believe to be true about you?
Or you can use what he said for me?

1._____
2._____
3._____

What is God's vision or message for you?
Get still and listen for the voice or message. What is coming through?
Or what passage from my entry spoke to you?

Day 12: April 22, 2011

Taking Stock:

- Good friends who stand by me
- A hug (a good one)
- The sunrise
- The sunset
- The voice inside my head that loves me
- The smell of fresh cut grass
- An organized space
- Helping others get organized (the Aha! moment)
- Falling in love with myself
- When my heart overflows with love
- Playing with a puppy or Jack
- A smile from a stranger (when they really see you)
- Knowing someone without ever having met them before
- That instant connection with another person
- An old friend
- When someone really knows me and loves me anyway
- Being on stage teaching
- Trusting myself
- A cold beer on a really hot day
- The coolness of the ocean
- Swimming in a lake
- Cartwheels
- Laughter
- Friends
- Game night with friends
- Celebrating my successes (no matter how small)
- This process (even when I fight it, it always warms my heart)
- Knowing that I'm connected

God's Belief System:

- I am open to change.
- The world is here to serve me.
- People are coming out of the woodwork.
- I have the best friends.
- I'm so fortunate. Things always work out for my best.
- I'm courageous, creative and compassionate.
- Money flows to me easily.
- Whatever I focus on expands, and my business is booming.
- I'm in excellent health and I take great care of my body, mind & spirit.
- Love is all around me.
- We are all meant for happiness.
- Love is my greatest expression.
- I am grateful for my life.
- I am blessed.
- I am protected and provided for.
- I love easily without reservation.

God's Vision or Message:

You are loved. There is nothing you need. Opening your heart again is okay. Trust: that is the key to life. Trust yourself to open and love without holding back. Be in a state of peace and deep connection to me. There is no other place you need to look in your life. Sometimes you get off track thinking you need to plan ahead. While I appreciate your efforts, everything you need is provided for you.

You are wonderful and kind. You love to help others. Let me help you. Let our time together bring you closer to what you've been looking for. It all begins and ends in silence, that echo of a voice that can only be heard when you are listening. So much of what society does deadens that voice. People keep their lives so full and so busy that there is no time to slow down and hear. It doesn't have to be so hard. Just relax into the silence and stillness and hear my voice, trusting all is okay. It's always scary doing something new, but before you know it, new isn't new any longer. Then it gets comfortable, and you'll wonder why it took you so long in the first place.

You are a bright shining light. Trust that everyone will do right by you. If they don't, something will come from that experience to serve your highest good.

Stay focused on my vision for you, and now shift your behaviors to come into alignment with what you are hearing from me. Your results will then catapult beyond your wildest expectations.

Day 12 Exercise

Taking Stock:
What are 3 things/moments that take your breath away or have you pause with appreciation?

1._____
2._____
3._____

God's Belief System:
What are 3 things God would believe to be true about you?
Or you can use what he said for me?

1._____
2._____
3._____

What is God's vision or message for you?
Get still and listen for the voice or message. What is coming through?
Or what passage from my entry spoke to you?

Day 13: April 23, 2011

Taking Stock:

- The caress of the wind on my skin
- A hummingbird greeting me at my front door
- The sound a wind chime makes
- A random conversation with a stranger
- The feel of the sun warming my body
- Watching someone who has mastered something
- Dolphins and whales
- The strength of the ocean
- A full moon
- My girlfriends
- Knowing that I'm loved
- Art
- Cirque du Soleil
- The ballet
- Sitting with a daisy or flower
- Watching the water flow by
- Remembering that I am connected
- My girlfriend telling me that I'm important in her life.

God's Belief System:

- I am honest, kind, loving and loyal.
- The best things happen for me.
- I am so successful, and my business is thriving.
- I see the best in people.
- My heart is open, and I care deeply for others.
- I trust my life is unfolding perfectly.
- I am blessed.
- The world is conspiring for my greatest good.
- I always act in the highest good.
- Others' lives are better for knowing me.

- I love my life.
- I am connected and tapped in.
- I focus only on what I choose to create.
- I take great care of my body, mind and spirit.
- I see beauty in everything.
- I hear music in the day unfolding.
- Abundance is everywhere.
- I am protected, loved and adored.

God's Vision or Message:

You know what needs to be done. I realize you are resisting because this is starting to take off. You now have others enrolled, and it's happening quickly. Your only requirement is to breathe and keep the lines of communication open. There is only resistance in your own mind. You create all of your own barriers in everything you do. Only you can stop yourself from having anything.

The beauty of our arrangement is that you are living my vision of your life, my belief system. You are giving up your belief system just for a short time. Fall in love with your life and with every single thing you do.

Life is to be savored. There is so much bounty, beauty and wonder to behold. If you ever doubt that, just watch a child take life in. You'll see a true reflection of what's happening. Watch the wonder and discovery in their eyes. Babies are the best... they only experience without judgment, for they haven't bought into the conditioning yet, and they see with unfiltered eyes.

Love yourself as I love you. Can you feel it? Do you get a sense of what's possible? You are sticking with it. I am so proud of you. I feel your desire to pull away, your eyes are now opening, and you have new eyes to see. Sometimes it's too much to take in.

You are on such a wonderful journey. It is rich with possibilities! Go and laugh today and find me in those moments of pure joy. I'm in every one, all of them: the innocent moments, as well as the sharing of love between two or more people.

Close your eyes and find the stillness. And in that stillness, come and dance with me. Celebrate our joining together, to live your fullest life yet.

Remember your dreams from when you were young. They are there to guide you.

Stay in this moment with me, now and always. If you get off track, go to your breath, and find your way back.

Day 13 Exercise

Taking Stock:
What are 3 things/moments that take your breath away or have you pause with appreciation?

1._____
2._____
3._____

God's Belief System:
What are 3 things God would believe to be true about you?
Or you can use what he said for me?

1._____
2._____
3._____

What is God's vision or message for you?
Get still and listen for the voice or message. What is coming through?
Or what passage from my entry spoke to you?

Day 14: April 24, 2011

Taking Stock:

- The birds singing me awake
- Waking up early
- The early morning stretch
- Sharing a meal with friends
- My friends
- Being involved in a conscious community
- Hummingbirds
- Feeling my heart open
- Holding hands
- The possibility at the start of the day
- This process
- A great kiss
- Loving myself
- Trusting myself
- A great workout
- Doing the right thing
- Game night with friends
- The sound of the ocean
- A hike in the mountains
- Being out in nature
- A sweet dream

God's Belief System:

- I am healthy and vibrant.
- My heart is open.
- Amazing people surround me.
- I am blessed.
- I am loved, valued and adored.
- I trust myself.
- People are out for my highest good.

- I come from contribution.
- Everything I need is provided before I ask.
- The universe always is supporting me.
- I'm always in the right place and the right time.
- I am an outstanding presenter, trainer and speaker.
- I take great care of my body, mind and spirit.
- I am always connected.
- My energy is high and never runs out, especially when I'm tapped in.
- Money flows to me easily and in all ways.
- I love to manage my money and watch it grow.
- I use my money to help others too!
- I am a gift.
- I trust God and myself at all times.
- I am willing to show up fully in every moment.
- I love myself.
- I know my worth and am compensated highly for it.

God's Vision or Message:

Welcome back, even though you've been tuning in all day. Yes, it's time to take this process up a notch. You are doing terrifically. You are exactly where I want you to be. Remember this next phase is all about discovery of what could happen if you believe what I believe about you. It's time to take the actions I would have you take. This way, you'll know the full effects of what's possible with this process.

You need to be brave and you need to manage your energy. Spend more time reading or listening if you must, in order to do whatever it takes to shift into my behaviors for you vs. your own behaviors. If you are really going to embrace this process, then it's time for the next level. Remember, it's all a game of what could happen. It's critical that you stay in wonderment. You'll need to tap into extra energy in the beginning because you are paving a new wave of thought. This extra push will be necessary only for the beginning. Stay focused on what I want for you. If you get nervous or freaked out, step out and connect back with me. Then start up again.

You are doing amazingly! It's gaining momentum, and your default behavior is to stop it. Remember, that's just a way you used to keep yourself safe. You are and have always been safe. You'll do great. Keep up the good work. I'm so proud of you.

You are such a love, wanting to reach out and help others. You have such a big heart and innocence in the way you love, too. It's quite beautiful to watch it develop. I'm happy you retained some of your innocence. That's why this process is finally working, because you got really honest about yourself and what you were up to.

Your business will thrive. Take my word for it. You are ready to receive what you've always wanted, and you aren't scared anymore. You'll still have lingering fears, but they no longer apply to you, and they will fade over time. You are remarkable and amazing! I love you so very much.

Day 14 Exercise

Taking Stock:
What are 3 things/moments that take your breath away or have you pause with appreciation?

1._____
2._____
3._____

God's Belief System:
What are 3 things God would believe to be true about you?
Or you can use what he said for me?

1._____
2._____
3._____

What is God's vision or message for you?
Get still and listen for the voice or message. What is coming through?
Or what passage from my entry spoke to you?

Day 15: April 25, 2011

Taking Stock:

- Reading my previous entries
- Believing that God's vision will work
- Feeling my heart overflow with love
- Hearing the joy from others doing this process
- Sharing this possibility with others
- My body tingling with energy
- The morning sun filtering into my room
- The birds singing me awake
- Knowing that I am powerful
- Dinners with Miriam
- Taking myself to a movie
- Watching the leaves blow in the wind
- Being present
- Meeting new people
- Helping a friend
- Silence
- Relaxing on the Miracle Ball (letting my body unwind the stress)
- Lucille Ball's quote – I am not funny. What I am is brave! (every time it gets me)
- Having the best, most amazing friends
- Taking a walk on a sunny day
- Trusting myself
- Feeling the wind on my skin
- A great workout
- Connecting with another person (heart to heart)
- Being appreciated
- Appreciating others

God's Belief System:

- There is so much to love in this life.
- I meet the best people wherever I go.
- I see the best in those around me.
- Cheerleading others to success is my natural inclination.
- I love my life, every part of it.
- I am blessed now and always.
- I am safe, happy and vibrantly healthy.
- My heart is open, and I follow its lead.
- People are rallying to help me succeed.
- Everything I need is provided before I ask.
- I have the most amazing friends and family.
- I trust myself, my inner voice.
- I trust God.
- Abundance is everywhere.
- I manage my money with ease, and it's growing exponentially.
- I use my "Give" money to help others.
- I am always in the right place at the right time.
- I am safe.
- I follow my inner voice.
- I am vibrantly healthy; my body is fit, strong and lean.
- I see opportunity everywhere I go.
- I trust God's vision for my life.

God's Vision or Message:

See what happens when you let go and let me work? It's only the beginning. The floodgates are opening. Make sure you have your time allocated properly. Looks like in order to read the whole book you are writing, you need to wake up earlier. Did you notice how reading that first thing in the morning shifted you right into the flow of us working together?

Yes, I did.

Also keep it with you, and you'll see how it is unfolding. Also remember the idea that came to you about reading it aloud in your own voice so you can create an audio file of it and load it up on your IPod and take it with you when you hike?

Yes, I got that.

Well I felt it best to have you write it down now, because things will be flowing easily, and you'll get overwhelmed if you rely on your memory since this isn't fully coming from you as much as through you. Some will stick, but writing will be best.

I know that to be true. When I was reading my past entries I couldn't remember writing them and I kept thinking wow, this is brilliant.

It's just the beginning, I know I keep saying it, but it's true. Remember to stay in a place of showing up to see what happens. Don't limit me by your thinking or coming to our conversation with your own ideas, which will affect the results. Just stay in a sense of wonder and watch it unfold. That way you give me more room to work through you. Place your focus on what will happen. Keep asking yourself, "What could happen if I just show up for the next 30 days? What's possible?" If you continue questioning with an open heart, then I have room to work through you and show you.

This is getting better each day; our connection is growing stronger. Lean on that connection in the moments you feel yourself wavering to follow through with this process. It's a day-by-day experiment, so keep focused on what's possible... today.

Who will I meet? How much business can I conduct? What choices can I make for my highest good?

I've got your answers. Let those be the things you give your mind to chew on. It doesn't need to work anything out. Keep it centered on questions. That's the expansion we are looking for.

Today is a big day. It's your first day speaking from alignment and living from total alignment. So far, you are investing your time in this conversation. That is excellent. Trust that whatever you need will unfold from here.

This journey is spectacular. Keep your vision on it. You are beautiful, funny, smart, sexy and such a light in this world. It's time more people get the benefit of your light. You are exactly where you need to be! When you stop thinking and stick with writing, the messages come faster and clearer. Good for you. You can quickly get off track, but can come back to this. Our connection is growing. Before you know it, we'll have this connection all day long. We'll have a dialogue that doesn't need to be centered just in moments of sitting together. It will begin to become a way of life for you. You will always be connected, moment-by-moment, checking in to see what's possible or what is the best course.

Does this mean I shouldn't plan out my day?

Not at all. Having an idea of where you are going and what needs to be done is critical. A plan can guide you. It can also give your brain the ability to measure your progress and daily actions against something.

Can you give me more details on how to flow through my day?

Sure. Starting the day is most important. Take a break and come back. Eat, and then we'll talk.

Not only did you feed yourself but also you fed a squirrel. How did that feel?

It was amazing to watch him come right up close to meet me, get the almonds, eat them, and go bury them for later. It was sweet, and it felt good to be of service, even to a squirrel. We share the same address for the most part. It's about helping out another being. He wasn't really scared of me either.

Planning your day is a very good idea, yet it doesn't leave time for those kinds of moments to show up. Have an idea of how you want your day to unfold, but let inspiration guide you as well. Don't become so married to an idea that you become rigid and fixate on it. Allow for the possibility of something else to show up and trust that all will get done. I also understand the concept of being under a deadline to finish a project, so all things have their own time element. But, even that idea is fluid. More importantly, allow for whatever happens to happen. Trust your guidance in doing things exactly at the right time for you, even though for this process, there really is no "time." There is just this moment. So moment by moment, check in with yourself and see what is needed for you to be in alignment with your highest possible good. Keep yourself centered in the questions to keep you on track.

Right now, my vision is for you to get your details in alignment with what's coming. The process will unfold quickly. I'm looking forward to this message getting out. Yes, you have other messages, but this message is critical for the greater good. It will be a way for you to express yourself, to be of service and to help others. Yes, you have other things you want to do to express yourself and to be of service, but just know that this process will help pave the way for all of those other things to reveal themselves and evolve.

It's so much bigger than you think it's going to be. You are creating a possibility for others to test for themselves. Some will; some won't. But, it's not about reaching everyone right now. There are those that are looking for this message. They'll find it. The beauty is that you are creating a platform where everyone who follows this process will get to share their experiences, if they choose to. You are offering others a way to play, discover and listen for that voice within themselves... a way for them to listen for me. That voice does not exclude anyone; I don't exclude anyone. I love all of you just the same.

There is only love, and when you remember that, you will shift how you interact with those around you. You'll start exuding love and appreciation for those in your life, and you'll start to lift them up. In turn, you'll lift yourself up.

This is about inclusion and creating a community, but not resting in that community. Rather, you are constantly evolving into the next higher version of who you are. When we align too much with one group, we begin to alienate others. That's not what this is about. This is about creating a group of people whose, sole purpose is to support each other in realizing their highest vision... my highest vision, for their lives. We are all on the same path of discovery. It's just that some involve hard work and suffering as part of their path, while this process about play and discovery. Which do you prefer?

Play and discovery, of course!

Which is why nothing worked for you prior to this process. Everything you tried before involved work instead of play. And work was shrouded and veiled by conversations of right and wrong.

When you were a child, I gave you the gift to play your life as it unfolds. However, you were trained to unlearn that gift. This process is about getting you back to playing. That's why you did cartwheels, stopped on the grass and fed a squirrel. This process is opening you back to the gift you knew from the beginning. Play your life as it unfolds. Breathe and discover. That's all you have to do. I love you.

Day 15 Exercise

Taking Stock:
What are 3 things/moments that take your breath away or have you pause with appreciation?

1._____
2._____
3._____

God's Belief System:
What are 3 things God would believe to be true about you?
Or you can use what he said for me?

1._____
2._____
3._____

What is God's vision or message for you?
Get still and listen for the voice or message. What is coming through?
Or what passage from my entry spoke to you?

Day 16: April 26, 2011

Taking Stock:

- My mom doing this process
- Marjean getting downloads & insights
- My friends getting tangible results with this experiment
- A cool spring evening
- Walking downtown and checking out the homes along the way
- See possibilities show up
- A smile
- A kiss
- A great hug
- Laughing
- A sleep over at a girlfriend's house
- A great night's sleep
- That early morning stretch
- A cup of tea first thing in the am
- That feeling of love brewing in my heart
- Trusting in God
- Knowing everything will work out
- Great compliments (take my breath away)
- The singing of the birds
- The sound of someone mowing the lawn
- The laughter of kids swimming in the lake
- The sound of splashing in the lake
- Breakfasts with everyone at Spofford lake cottage
- Spending a whole day in my bathing suit, going in and out of the water
- Vacationing with girlfriends
- Training with Marjean, especially in Malaysia
- Water polo in Malaysia
- The feeling of being on a team
- Helping others
- Random acts of kindness

- Sweet smell of night blooming jasmine all around my house
- Feeling the grass between my toes
- Meeting a stranger and having a great conversation
- That fact that this list is easy to build
- More moments of being present
- Stillness
- Talking with God

God's Belief System:

- I am the best person I can be.
- I love with my whole being.
- I see the best in others.
- Appreciating someone feels like oxygen.
- I love my life.
- I am blessed now and always.
- The world is conspiring for my greatest good.
- People are coming out of the woodwork to help me succeed.
- My clients are the best, I'm so grateful to work with wonderful people.
- My business is booming.
- I have a great team supporting my business.
- I am amazing, wonderful, beautiful and loved.
- I am always in the right place at the right time.
- I take excellent care of my body, mind and spirit.
- I love this process and am excited to see what shows up.
- I am strong, confident and compassionate leader.
- I trust God and me.
- I live my days fully.
- I see miracles throughout the day.
- I am worthy of the best life has to offer.
- I am the best person to deliver this message.

God's Vision or Message:

Something unique happened tonight. While talking with Marjean she said, "Write this down. I have a message for you." So I did.

What God said through Marjean:

"You are causing a molecular shift in people. You've come through and blown the entire structure up, the belief system, the patterning, and the chemical make-up of the humanness of the being. You've blown it into oblivion, and it is now going to go through a shift of reorganization to create an entirely different operating system."

Wow, thanks for talking through someone else to let the bigger picture through. I apologize for limiting you with my fear.

You never have to apologize to me. The message never shifts. What you are able to hear and receive will shift and open. You are exactly where you need to be. You are getting ready for what's coming. Trust me when I say that you've got a lot of things ahead of you, and we are just scratching the surface.

Is it arrogant that I'm writing that I've got big plans?

No, it isn't. You aren't saying it. I am. Let people think what they will. You stay your course, and everything will fall into place. Just stay focused on what's right in front of you. Keep your eyes down and do each step to the best of your ability. I know your heart, your hopes and your fears. I understand what you are going through, and it's important for you to be the lead. It's not about following anymore or sitting in the back row. You must stand up, raise your hand and get the word out.

This is a beautiful opportunity for many to open to their connection with me. They all have the connection. But some are listening and others aren't. Even some that are listening aren't acting on what they are hearing. Remember how long it took for you to act on this message. Didn't you have to injure your foot to slow you down long enough to listen and take action?

Sometimes you move so fast that it's difficult to connect with me. You've led a fast, loud and very busy life as many others have. Many of you fill up the silence with so much chaos and noise, which often doesn't allow for my voice to be heard and for us to have a conversation. And this is a conversation... our conversation.

Everyone has the same opportunity for a conversation. There is a myth that I only speak through prophets or to those in a church. That isn't true. That's just manipulation and not intentional for many who are acting this way. They are just adopting beliefs of those who came before them and are doing what they feel is right. You don't need to go through anyone to ever communicate with me. You need only to create an opening and stick with it long enough for us to build rapport. You have enough experience to trust what you are receiving.

I personally don't want to get into a religious conversation.

Thank you for speaking up. For now, we'll put it aside until you feel stronger in these messages you are receiving. Just breathe. Thank you, for not editing too much of what I am saying. It's important that people understand how simple it is and how much benefit they will receive from just taking on the experiment for 30 days.

You are wonderful, remarkable and you are a gift. Don't worry about the future. It's not here yet. Don't worry about what has yet to happen. It's a moment-to-moment conversation that unfolds. Just stay patient and don't try to skip ahead. Everything is unfolding perfectly and at the right time.

Get some rest, and we'll talk first thing in the A.M. Sleep well.

Day 16 Exercise

Taking Stock:
What are 3 things/moments that take your breath away or have you pause with appreciation?

1._____
2._____
3._____

God's Belief System:
What are 3 things God would believe to be true about you?
Or you can use what he said for me?

1._____
2._____
3._____

What is God's vision or message for you?
Get still and listen for the voice or message. What is coming through?
Or what passage from my entry spoke to you?

_____
_____
_____
_____
_____
_____
_____
_____
_____
_____
_____

Day 17: April 27, 2011

Taking Stock:

- Walking with ease
- Loving with my whole heart
- Getting caught up in this moment
- A really great hug
- A sunny summer day
- Letting the sun soak into my skin
- The sound of waterfalls
- Laughter of children
- Watching a dog roll in the grass
- Laying on the grass
- Sitting in a tree
- My dear friends
- My clients, I have the best clients
- The sound of a wind chime
- Making friends with the dog next door
- A comfy chair and a cup of tea
- Floating on the water
- Sitting in a hot spring
- Feeling of floating
- Flying Trapeze
- The feeling of being physically spent from a great workout
- The twinkle in someone's eye
- A stranger saying hello and really connecting
- Random acts of kindness
- Helping a stranger in need
- Drumming, drum circles
- Dancing
- Learning specific dances
- Learning in general... I love to learn

God's Belief System:

- I am beautiful, confident and powerful.
- I radiate joy and laughter wherever I go.
- The world is conspiring for my highest good.
- People go out of their way to help me.
- I am blessed.
- I am always in the right place at the right time.
- I meet the greatest people.
- I have the best experiences because I see the good.
- Money flows to me easily.
- I manage my money with enthusiasm, and it's growing exponentially.
- I bring out the best in people.
- I create amazing friendships and business relationships with ease and joy.
- I love my life.
- Clients are lining up to work with me.
- I have a terrific team that helps me in my business.
- My body is fit, lean and healthy.
- I take right action moment by moment.
- I pick things up quickly and assimilate them easily.
- I am an amazing modeler.

God's Vision or Message:

Your journey is spectacular. Lead your life with your heart at all times. Your heart is connected with me and knows what's best for you. Trust in that voice that is guiding you. Instead of tuning it out, listen and act on it. The only reason you get pulled off track is because you feel the pull to be stronger than you. It never is. You are giving your power away. There is such a grace and beauty about you. The only thing you need to do is reach out and live it. You already are everything you need to be.

Also for the next few days together, give up your addiction to what you've done in the past. It's funny...this "comparison addiction" of yours is gnawing at you. Trust that the voice you hear, my voice, will be your compass to get you where you want to ultimately be.

You have, as always, many things on your plate. You have time for everything you want to do. Just make sure you are doing it from an inspired place or otherwise you'll be sabotaging your energy, and then you'll take yourself out.

We keep talking about the next phase. Here is the thing: stay on the phase you are in and go after it with everything you have. Align yourself with it, and then you'll be able to draw it to you instead of working yourself so hard to get what you want. It's a conversation of finesse.

You are feeling disconnected from me. It's okay. Just create the situation you want to live out and do whatever it takes to live into it.

My ego keeps saying my channel is blocked.

From now on, do these in the mornings: create a time where you are feeling in the flow and make this a priority. Only write our conversation down, and leave the bullet point sections for later.

This is your time to awaken and to help others become awake. You have a large goal in front of you. This is an amazing opportunity to put your trust and faith to the test. I want the best for you, as much as you'll allow times a thousand.

Day 17 Exercise

Taking Stock:
What are 3 things/moments that take your breath away or have you pause with appreciation?

1._____
2._____
3._____

God's Belief System:
What are 3 things God would believe to be true about you?
Or you can use what he said for me?

1._____
2._____
3._____

What is God's vision or message for you?
Get still and listen for the voice or message. What is coming through?
Or what passage from my entry spoke to you?

Day 18: April 28, 2011

Taking Stock:

- A sunny day
- Brightening my mom's day
- Finding a movie that speaks this message
- Buying that movie for mom to pick up
- Random acts of kindness
- A cup of tea
- Seeing Marjean off at the airport
- Feeding the squirrel
- Making healthy meals for myself
- Bouncing on my Cellerciser
- A hug... a good one
- Knowing someone is thinking about me
- Talking to a new client
- Planning a vacation
- Feeling loved
- Bonding with my neighbor's dog, Abby
- Knowing my value
- Feeling heat when it's cold
- A cool breeze when it's warm
- The wind chime
- The smell of night blooming jasmine
- How doing this list puts me into the flow
- Feeling connected
- Appreciating those I love
- Taking care of the details of my life, always lifts my spirits
- A smile
- A laugh

God's Belief System:

- I am a good person.
- I love to help others.
- The world is always conspiring for my highest good.
- I meet the best people wherever I go.
- I love my life.
- I feel strong, fit, and lean.
- I take great care of my body.
- I am blessed.
- Whatever I need is provided before I ask.
- I am happy.
- I have amazing friends and family.
- My clients are fantastic, appreciative and refer me often.
- My business is thriving.
- I am compassionate.
- I am kind, loving, and loyal.
- I am beautiful, funny and sexy.
- I feel my best right now.
- I care deeply for others.
- I share my heart easily.
- Cheerleading for others brings me great joy.
- I deserve the best life can offer.
- I receive love and compliments with ease and joy.
- I take right action daily moment-by-moment.
- I love to be active fit and adventurous.
- I love to be outdoors in nature.

God's Vision or Message:

Every person can make the largest difference. It's not about setting out to change the world; rather it's about being the best version of you in each moment and sharing your heart and passion with others. This naturally grows and expands to everyone you are around and to everything of which you are a part.

You are right on track. This journey with me is about letting go your self-judgment. Some days you feel you do better than others. Your addiction to comparison and the pressure you are putting on yourself to be an example for others is too much right now. Stay in the enjoyment of this process that is unfolding for you. There is so much to be appreciated. Stay focused here, this moment, on what needs to happen next. Stay connected with me and in the flow.

You have the ability to light up others. You bond easily, and people open up to you. This gift you have is your opening to share this message. People are searching for that connection with me. There is so much propaganda around how and when I show up. I am always here for everyone in every moment. You don't have to go anywhere to be with or converse with me. Some days are more challenging than others. For you, my dear, it's the quiet of the morning or the evening.

Life isn't about struggle. Ever. It's abundant and full of possibility. So many of you get stuck in the feeling of disconnection or the idea that life must inherently be hard, or it couldn't be that easy. It is that easy! Only your conditioning makes it otherwise. If you manage your personal energy and monitor what goes into your mind, then you can consciously create your reality as you see fit. If you don't monitor your thoughts and what you put in, you'll be creating other people's visions for your life. What fun is that?

This shift that is taking place is starting to happen at a faster pace. Just refine what you are doing with the participants of the experiment. Just let them come in and play. Did you like that I found you a movie today that speaks directly into this?

What is your vision specifically for my life?

You are to teach, train and wake people up. Show them how much fun they can have by just allowing themselves to show up as they are. Help them develop their communication with me. This paradigm shift is taking place. You will be part of the new movement of thought, sharing this message and laughter to help others.

I know I'm limiting you out of fear of what the bigger grander vision really is.

You won't be the only one. You have created fear out of dreaming big for yourself. My dream is so much bigger.

Day 18 Exercise

Taking Stock:
What are 3 things/moments that take your breath away or have you pause with appreciation?

1._____
2._____
3._____

God's Belief System:
What are 3 things God would believe to be true about you?
Or you can use what he said for me?

1._____
2._____
3._____

What is God's vision or message for you?
Get still and listen for the voice or message. What is coming through?
Or what passage from my entry spoke to you?

_____
_____
_____
_____
_____
_____
_____
_____
_____
_____
_____

Day 19: April 29, 2011

Taking Stock:

- A sunny day
- A good friend
- My mom doing this process
- Loving my work again
- Trusting my intuition
- Seeing a hawk soar today
- Talking to a senior man and taking the time to listen
- Dan sending me good energy to start my day
- My mom taking care of Jack
- Sending mom money for Jack
- Getting an email from a potential client
- Catching up with Marjean
- Putting the windows down on a hot day
- Driving along the ocean
- Laughing
- The possibility of something new happening
- Bouncing for 20 minutes, and I can (my foot is getting better)
- Feeling healthy
- Seeing a photo of someone laughing
- Singing happy birthday to Bennett and having him tap his foot along with me
- Being included as a part of someone else's family
- Talking with my Aunt Lucy

God's Belief System:

- My success is and always has been right here in this moment.
- I am an amazing businesswoman.
- People go out of their way to help me.
- I know I am loved, valued and adored.
- My life is wonder-full.

- The world is conspiring for my greatest good.
- Whatever I need is provided before I even ask.
- I am happy, confident, smart, funny, kind and loving.
- I'm an amazing friend.
- I love with my whole heart.
- I can have anything I want.
- God is my best friend.
- I trust myself.
- I see the best in people.
- I act in the moment for my highest good.
- I am productive and disciplined.

God's Vision or Message:

You weren't created to be in struggle. This life was designed for you to create by using what you don't want to create what you do want. Though it seems you keep forgetting how simple it really can be. It's a matter of adjusting your focus.

I want for you happiness, great happiness, joy and wonder at the beauty of life unfolding around you. You can be whatever you choose to be. You are brilliant and magnificent. There is nothing you need to do from this point on. As you are in this moment, you have everything you need.

The addiction to comparison is keeping you feeling disconnected. Things, status, and wealth are not true signs of you living in alignment or ways to measure yourself by. If you live your life by comparing those things, you'll never feel complete. There is always someone in your estimation further ahead or behind you. Yet there is only this life unfolding. Once you realize and know that you need nothing more to have whatever you desire, you will begin to create from a place of abundance knowing everything is at your disposal.

When you find yourself comparing, stop in that moment, breathe and recite this: *I was complete the day I was born, everything I need is within me.*

Then focus on what you want to be creating, keep your eyes firmly upon your experience. Take time every day to keep this connection with me. You will be tapping into that knowledge.

Focus is the power of creation. You have heard this. You have the power to control your focus at all times. It's developing the discipline to train your focus to stay firmly upon what you want to create, not the HOW to create, just what you want to create. Life is a menu, and you are placing your order by where you choose to focus your attention. If you have an unwanted experience, be grateful for it, for it has given you knowledge of what you do want. Put your attention immediately back on what you do want, for you are always creating moment by moment, and if you spend too much time on the things that aren't working out you let those experiences take root in your life.

If you don't have the job or money that you want, use the gift of that knowledge to clear up what you do want and put your mind on it.

There will be a lag time before what you want shows up. During this time, trust that what you are creating is on its way. Hold your course and keep your focus. Before you know it, your life will reflect what it is that you want.

Remember, once things come into alignment; keep your attention on what you are creating. Once you look up, look around and take stock, your comparison addiction will start judging your results and knock you out of the flow. Be appreciative of what you've accomplished and know that it is *a moment-by-moment creation. We are constantly looking into a reflection of who we are being. Change is inevitable. Be gentle with yourself. Like any true athlete, it takes time to build your endurance. And you do so by training, intensive training and focus.*

You will have amazing moments when you are challenged. Welcome all of it as your life. In those challenging times, just love yourself, pick yourself back up and get back into the flow of creation. NO judgment, NO blame. It's all the game of life, and it's all part of the process of creating stamina. Everything serves you. Everything does.

Day 19 Exercise

Taking Stock:
What are 3 things/moments that take your breath away or have you pause with appreciation?

1._____
2._____
3._____

God's Belief System:
What are 3 things God would believe to be true about you?
Or you can use what he said for me?

1._____
2._____
3._____

What is God's vision or message for you?
Get still and listen for the voice or message. What is coming through?
Or what passage from my entry spoke to you?

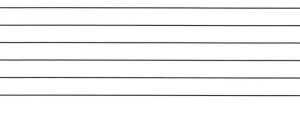

Day 20: April 30, 2011

Taking Stock:

- Listening to people laugh
- A great kiss
- A great hug
- Being wrapped in someone's arms
- Feeling my heart expand with love
- Singing in front of a crowd
- Creating a laughter circle
- Meeting new people
- Putting on a dress and feeling great in it
- Feeling sexy
- A drive on summer's day with the windows down

God's Belief System:

- I am sweet, kind, happy, enthusiastic, funny, loving, and compassionate.
- I am love.
- Everything is love.

God's Vision or Message:

My life is working out beautifully. I know that it's scary to shift. I'm living it. However, I believe the truth about myself as God sees it.

Wow, my ego is taking over on my "to do" list.

It's not your ego. What I am asking is for you to get the details of your life in order. Take the time to map out yourself and see what you come up with. Record your book in your own voice and play that throughout the day. Imprint my words into your mind by speaking them to yourself. Let my words override anything you've got going on. You are creating momentum, everything is unfolding just as it is, and you are doing amazingly. Take care of the details as you go. I keep creating open space in your schedule to give you the time to get into alignment. You know that I'm right here. You can feel me. This is your time. There is nothing you need to do, no one you have to be. All you have to do is show up exactly as you are. You aren't perfect, in your eyes. That doesn't matter. The fact that you are struggling to shift will be more relatable than if you just shifted easily. I know your habits are strong; you are stronger. You know this. It's the fear of what comes next.

Let's talk about that, shall we?

You have a beautiful life waiting for you, so many people are asking for help. You are the answer.

Woah! That's ridiculous! Me? Who am I to say that?

You aren't saying that. You are still too scared to believe it fully, so you limit what I am capable of. What if you feel it to be true? This process is the opportunity so many are waiting for in order to develop their own connection with me, to develop their own listening. It took you years to really listen to me. Now there is the possibility of this message getting out. It's not about you being the perfect example. The more you are honest about how challenging this is for you, the easier it will be for others.

I can see the benefits of what's possible and see the new vision for my life. It's like a veil is being lifted. I've always been able to see it.

It's just about the courage to walk the path. You have the courage and you know you do. You are safe. Trust me.

Look at that; right there... your hesitation. This is the moment we've been working towards. That belief, that block. This is the place where you seem to stumble over and over again.

Yes, I am right here. This time, we are walking together. I have your hand in all of this. This time we are in alignment. You are getting so much better every day. You are strengthening your spirit and self each day. You are here. The fear feels like a fire, but is not a true fire... it's an illusion, one cast to keep you small and safe. You needed it when you were young in order to survive. You aren't that little girl anymore that has to hide herself in plain sight. You are breaking through your protective shell. The light is coming in. Your light is beginning to shine through even though you still make attempts to hide it. You are becoming too bright to go back. You are exactly where you need to be. I'm so proud of you. It's important because it gives you compassion for what others could be going through. It's a very simple process. Yet many struggle with it when, in truth, the struggle is self-created. That's what you are here to know, deep into the fiber of your being. With me, there is no struggle. There is only abundance, love, and joy. Anything other than that is not the truth. It's your conditioning, mind, or ego playing their role to keep you safe. Follow your heart. I'm right here. Your heart will guide you home.

Rest and return; play and have fun. Your life is meant to be fun, happy and full of joy! Not everything is supposed to go your way. Allow those things to be there and use them for their purpose to guide you back into what you want. Then go back to the basics and continue on. You are doing great. You'll get exactly what you need to get. It doesn't have to be a magical transformation for you to know it to be true. All you truly want is to know me.

Yes, since this is all being said and done, I want to have a bountiful life, to take care of myself, help my mom and help others.

Do you want to win the lottery?

Is that a trick question?

No, I'm asking. Can you manage that kind of money yet? What would you do?

Get Mr. Money to help me immediately. I would do my jars and use it to help others. I want to help others. I know how it feels to be feeling down and blue, but still put on a smiling face.

Would you do that for me?

Yes!

Really? What if I don't win? Then all of this isn't true or real.

Do you honestly believe that?

No.

You want a test don't you? Isn't it about believing before seeing? Yes, it is.

Now I'm confused!

Exactly! You want so much to prove to others what this is. You want to make sure this is what you think it is. You don't need any of that. You only need to feel within your heart and trust what you feel. Does it feel possible? Does it feel true? Does this lift you up into the best version of yourself? That's all you need.

Winning the lottery would be undeniable proof.

Do you really think so? Others could always argue for or against it. I've given so many examples, and still it's not across-the-board proof for all. It doesn't matter what's happening for others; it matters what's happening for you. Do this process. Trust it, and that will be all you need. I am here for you. You still want lottery numbers, I feel it.

Yes I do!

Be patient. The lottery isn't always what you believe it to be. There are many versions of the lottery.

Go be yourself and trust in me. I love you, even in the moments you feel yourself to be unlovable. I still love you. Nothing can ever change that.

Day 20 Exercise

Taking Stock:
What are 3 things/moments that take your breath away or have you pause with appreciation?

1._____
2._____
3._____

God's Belief System:
What are 3 things God would believe to be true about you?
Or you can use what he said for me?

1._____
2._____
3._____

What is God's vision or message for you?
Get still and listen for the voice or message. What is coming through?
Or what passage from my entry spoke to you?

_____
_____
_____
_____
_____
_____
_____
_____
_____
_____
_____

Day 21: May 1, 2011

Taking Stock:

- A great night's sleep
- Loving myself
- Making new friends
- Sharing laughter with people
- Telling funny stories
- A group breakfast with friends
- A kiss
- A hug
- Knowing I am love
- Sharing my heart with others
- The birds singing
- Connecting with another person, deeply connecting
- A smile
- A warm embrace
- Swinging in a hammock
- Sitting in front of a fire
- Listening to other people tell funny stories
- Hanging out with a girlfriend
- Feeling my heart fill with love
- Liking someone and being myself with them
- Being called a girlfriend
- Calling AAA to help a girlfriend in need
- A sexy pair of jeans
- My girlfriends – I have the best girlfriends
- Hummingbirds
- Watching hawks soar overhead 2 of them

God's Belief System:

- I am happy.
- I have everything I'll ever need.

- My friends and family mean the most to me.
- I love my life.
- I trust that all is well always.
- My business is thriving.
- I love helping people.
- People go out of their way to help me.
- The world is conspiring for my greatest good.
- I share my heart with ease.
- My finances are growing and money flows to me easily.
- I deserve the best life has to offer.
- I can do anything.
- I can be anything.
- My heart is my greatest asset.
- My laughter is healing and I share it wherever I go.
- I am an amazing teacher, trainer and speaker.
- I have a great voice.
- I am a brilliant businesswoman.
- I create synergistic profitable teams.
- I love with my whole being.
- I care deeply for others.
- I trust in God.
- I trust my intuition and myself.

God's Vision or Message:

Today is an example of what life can be like. You are becoming so aware of dialogue, inner conversations and seeing the difference between my words and vision for you and other conversations from powerlessness and a feeling of lack. You are becoming aware. You are choosing to stand up and speak up for what you believe in. This project is just how you'll get your foot in the door.

I want to have significant financial results from this alignment with you.

It's not important to prove to others what you get out of this time with me.

For me it is... it's one thing to speak about shift but it's another to transform your financial abundance in one month or 6 weeks, depending on how you look at it.

All you have is time.

My wish for you is to really have you know me – to have you look at you from my eyes. You are brilliant and can do anything you dream of – I make no mistakes – you are beautiful. Teaching this work is going to be the next step. Sharing it, then teaching how to integrate or do this experiment. I love how you are checking in.

This process will transform the world. I want you to complete your days and then start writing up your process notes and arranging it. Also I will put you into alignment with the people necessary to create this into a book and design the cover for you.

Day 21 Exercise

Taking Stock:
What are 3 things/moments that take your breath away or have you pause with appreciation?

1._____
2._____
3._____

God's Belief System:
What are 3 things God would believe to be true about you?
Or you can use what he said for me?

1._____
2._____
3._____

What is God's vision or message for you?
Get still and listen for the voice or message. What is coming through?
Or what passage from my entry spoke to you?

Day 22: May 2, 2011

Taking Stock:

- My friend Miriam, love her
- A bright shiny day
- Being productive
- Hummingbirds
- When my car is warm from the sun
- Feeling healthy
- A quiet morning reading my pages
- Checking in with friends
- Sharing and celebrating successes with my friends
- Chatting with Marjean on the phone
- My clients, I have the best clients
- A massage
- A hug
- Emotional clearing work, I feel so light after
- My heart filled with love

God's Belief System:

- I am sweet, kind, funny and loved.
- I love my life.
- Each day is an opportunity to create my life anew.
- The world is conspiring for my greatest good.
- People always go out of their way to help me.
- There is so much good in this world.
- I thrive at all times.
- I am in excellent health.
- My heart is filled with love.
- My laugh is my greatest gift.
- I meet people easily and help them to see their highest good.
- I inspire people to go after what they want in their lives.
- I am happy, joyous, abundant and appreciative.

- I am blessed and provided for.
- I love helping others.
- I know how to put the right people together for the highest success of the individual and the whole.
- I bring like-minded people together.

God's Vision or Message:

You are such a trooper. You've had some challenges come your way, yet you still remain strong. I'm so proud of you. If you could only see yourself from my eyes there isn't anything you couldn't do. I believe in you and know what you are made of.

This is the challenge: as you start resonating with me you'll start noticing discrepancies in other people's dialogues. It's not for you to fix or teach them a new way of being. Rather just hold your own vibration and connection with me. Trust that you will call to you experiences that will serve you.

When a friend calls in need and wants you to back them up on the drama they are living out, it's okay to be compassionate for what they are feeling; yet you must hold your own alignment. Does it feel uplifting?

No it didn't. I kept reframing but it still went back into the wallowing hurtful energy.

Emotions are a part of being human. We all have them, it's important to use them for their intended purpose. Stifling them won't help; it's best to let them go. Watch children with their emotions they feel it for a moment or two and then they are onto something else. It's okay to feel what you are feeling; feel it and let it pass.

My focus is coming off of myself and more into supporting those on the journey with me, checking in to see how they are doing. I like to focus on others.

You are coming into alignment. Just stay centered in your heart. When your friends are in those types of positions wanting support, come from your heart and create a space for them to release their emotions where they feel safe doing so. You don't have to enroll with their line of thinking. Just stay in your center and share from there. Like I've said before, this path is messy. No one has a straight line. Mistakes are how we learn. Make them. Feel what you feel. Remember that if you stay in alignment with my vision of you, you'll come right back to center.

You are beautiful and an amazing friend. Support them in their highest visions of themselves. Most of all trust that you are being an example and don't need to guide other than with your own actions, for that speaks volumes without saying a word. When you are tapped in and connected, everyone knows. It's such a difference.

Day 22 Exercise

Taking Stock:
What are 3 things/moments that take your breath away or have you pause with appreciation?

1._____
2._____
3._____

God's Belief System:
What are 3 things God would believe to be true about you?
Or you can use what he said for me?

1._____
2._____
3._____

What is God's vision or message for you?
Get still and listen for the voice or message. What is coming through?
Or what passage from my entry spoke to you?

_____
_____
_____
_____
_____
_____
_____
_____
_____
_____
_____
_____

.

Day 23: May 3, 2011

Taking Stock:

- The sound of crickets
- A cool breeze coming through my window at night
- Being a friend
- Sharing my heart
- The freedom to express myself
- Being received
- Knowing I am loved
- My mom & Lucy praying for me
- My mom & Lucy praying for my friends
- A fan
- A loving god and knowing him
- A job well done
- My clients, I have the best clients
- A smile
- Laughter
- Talking about the things that bring me joy
- Sharing those things with others
- Being trusted
- Having someone really see me
- Thinking of my dad
- Lightning bugs
- The sound of frogs
- Going for a walk under a full moon
- Great music
- Dinner with friends
- Games with friends
- Building strong relationships with those I love
- My business thriving
- Staying focused on things that make my heart light up

God's Belief System:

- This is working.
- I am developing a relationship with God.
- I am loving, kind, loyal and care deeply for others.
- The world is good place full of possibility.
- I can be whomever I choose to be.
- I love with my whole heart.
- I am happy, funny, and enthusiastic.
- I see the best in people.
- People always help me out.
- People always show me their best.
- Manifesting is easy and effortless.
- My finances are growing and I'm able to help more people.
- My laughter is healing and I share liberally with others.
- I have the best life.
- I know I am loved, cared for and adored.
- I choose relationships where my spirits rise.
- I know my value.
- I know my heart and follow its lead.
- My life is abundant and I have time to do everything I want to do.

God's Vision or Message:

Tonight was a beautiful experience. Thank you for showing me what's possible.

Yes, it was a gift to watch the two of you together. You risked showing yourself and you were received. That is all I ask of you. Risk showing others what I know to be true about you. You are so beautiful, full of light and have a beautiful heart. You love without fear; you love with your whole being. Keep letting the love in and love out, share it liberally.

The amount of love you were feeling tonight is just the surface of what's possible. I know you were tapped in. Your energy is high and you both are feeling much better. This is just the iceberg of the experiment. It will change and evolve the more people do this. With every person putting their spin on the exchanges we have, it's going to be an amazing conversation of connection and contrast. Each interaction will be filled with what's possible for each person. Since you are all different everyone will have something a bit different from each other.

You have great courage going first and following through. Most times you are up late at night just to finish the journaling before bed. I'm so impressed with your commitment. When you commit to something you throw your whole being into it. I want you to be that committed to your own life and possibilities I see for you. You are growing your strength daily. It's such a pleasure to watch you open and grow. You are listening and now you hear me much more than before.

I want only happiness, joy, love, and laughter for you. Anything that isn't here to serve you will only aid you to get back to it. The awareness you are developing is that, even in the midst of crisis, you can keep your focus and center on joy, happiness, laughter, and love. You are growing stronger in this area. This is the gift you are bringing forth. You are also making an effort to stay connected with your newer friends and those on this journey with you. You are growing your conscious community and it's going to blossom and flourish seemingly overnight. Then all of you can come together and begin the path of co-creating from source energy, me.

The group of you will have a collective ripple effect and it's going to spread quickly. The reason it will be successful is you are opening people to cultivate their own experience and listen to the vision God has for them. You are only giving them initial guidelines and then they create what works for them.

It's critical now to think of how each person will be able to share their story and what medium you'll use to build a community and a connection for interaction and support.

You are one of the most incredible people I know. I am thoroughly impressed with your commitment, your style, your heart, and your spirit. You are exactly where I want you to be. This month is going to be spectacular for you. You'll be going through some changes physically, and emotionally as you move further into alignment with me. If you get nervous, just check in and I'll support you. Come back to this connection and we'll move through whatever is coming up for you. Start relying on me to help you when you are feeling strong emotions, it's a healing process and you are clearing the way for greater listening and manifesting.

The crickets are singing for you tonight. Listen to your impulses; they are me bubbling up messages to come through. The more you act on them the quicker you'll get results.

Have a good night's rest. See you in the morning!

Day 23 Exercise

Taking Stock:
What are 3 things/moments that take your breath away or have you pause with appreciation?

1._____
2._____
3._____

God's Belief System:
What are 3 things God would believe to be true about you?
Or you can use what he said for me?

1._____
2._____
3._____

What is God's vision or message for you?
Get still and listen for the voice or message. What is coming through?
Or what passage from my entry spoke to you?

_____
_____
_____
_____
_____
_____
_____
_____
_____
_____
_____
_____

Day 24: May 4, 2011

Taking Stock:

- Waking up refreshed
- An early morning workout
- Hearing the birds singing me awake
- Seeing a baby possum
- Good friends
- Seeing possibility open in my life
- My heart overflowing with love
- Sharing my successes with friends
- Making a point of calling friends each day
- Reconnecting with Linda
- Booking a new client
- Traveling for work
- Hero excited to see me when I arrive
- Dilys – she's an amazing friend
- Sitting in the warm sun
- A sweater when a chill is in the air
- Driving along the coast
- Listening to the waves crash
- Laying in the sand
- Walks along the beach
- Making someone else feel better
- Helping another
- Building richer relationships
- Doing something that scares me

God's Belief System:

- I know the world is filled with good people.
- I have the best experiences wherever I go.
- People go out of their way to help me.
- I am happy, loving, kind and loyal.

- I trust myself.
- I trust God.
- The world is full of beauty and possibility.
- Abundance is overflowing.
- My heart is open.
- Leading with my heart is the way to go.
- I live my life and use it up.
- I am a masterful creator and manifestor.
- We are meant to live joy-filled lives.
- I have the best friends and family.
- I have the best clients.
- I create amazing teams around me.
- I am joy, love, laughter and radiance.

God's Vision or Message:

Good job today. You took solid action and stayed in alignment. This is just the tip of the iceberg that we've got going. This project is about transforming lives and reaching people in an intimate way. It's time that people started listening to their own still voice within and looked within before consulting the external world. You are going to help people strengthen this relationship. GO speak and talk on this subject. Share your experience and touch people's hearts. It's time healing takes place and connects people together. You are the person to do this now using this medium.

When I listen to Abraham-Hicks I feel like their messages are much clearer than my own.

You are comparing yourself to them. This is about what you get, what you cultivate and develop. This is your private journey. You are the only one with your specific message. Many messages may be similar, yet there are people who are waiting to hear this message from you. Trust your instincts and take actions to follow them even if it feels bigger than you or out of place.

It's time for the paradigm to shift; time for people to be empowered again, time for people to develop their listening, time for change. Many new things are unfolding and managing this relationship is primary to all the others working effectively. Many want to go outside of themselves and it only keeps them spinning their wheels. Teach, share and spread the word.

You have access to key people who will help you with this getting into the right hands. You've seen the quality of life that's possible when you come from your heart and true offering and being received. It's miraculous. This is what we are developing, this possibility for others to live this way as well. Each day you'll get stronger and more in alignment to this vision, it's exciting.

You see how much you can create and how you've broken out of the mold for your financial life. Get your details in order; much will be happening at a quicker rate. It's just getting good. Keep up the good work by showing up and being here with me.

My vision for you is to have all the abundance you can receive and more, to be happy and play this life for the fullness possible for it. This life is my gift to you. Use it up. Enjoy every part of it. All of it is serving you. Experience as much of this life as you can squeeze in. There is so much available to you, seize it and appreciate it.

I am so happy to be in conversation with you, so happy to know you more fully.

Just breathe and breathe again that's all you have to do. You are equipped with everything else you need. It's all in front of you, reach out and grab it.

So often we look at what other people are doing and compare our results. This is about trusting the message you are getting is right for you. I know you feel that this should be more profound or that if others are going to read this you need to seem more than you are. You are perfect as you are. The message you are getting is exactly right for you. You are looking at my vision for you and as we go messages will get stronger. Trust that this is exactly what you are supposed to be getting. It's okay to have concerns but know that you are in this and it's working. The results are showing up, your evidence doesn't need to be spectacular. It's for you to remember that it's unfolding in your life. This is about what matters to you.

Day 24 Exercise

Taking Stock:
What are 3 things/moments that take your breath away or have you pause with appreciation?

1._____
2._____
3._____

God's Belief System:
What are 3 things God would believe to be true about you?
Or you can use what he said for me?

1._____
2._____
3._____

What is God's vision or message for you?
Get still and listen for the voice or message. What is coming through?
Or what passage from my entry spoke to you?

_____
_____
_____
_____
_____
_____
_____
_____
_____
_____
_____

Christiana Carter

Day 25: May 5, 2011

Taking Stock:

- A Reiki healing
- Reconnecting with 3 other friends
- Getting another check in the mail
- Celebrating my successes
- Being able to send mom money to splurge on Mother's Day
- The birds serenading me wherever I go
- Watching this project transform lives
- Adding two more people to my list of experimenters
- Being able to share my heart
- Opening my heart to Dan
- Being there for Michael and developing our friendship even further
- A smile from a stranger
- Letting the day take me wherever it wants to go
- Meeting new people

God's Belief System:

- I am being the catalyst to help other people.
- This experiment will transform countless lives for the better.
- I love my life.
- The world is full of abundance.
- Everyone is out to help me.
- I am blessed.
- My business is thriving and money is flowing in easily.
- I love to create.
- I manifest quickly and easily.
- Everything I need is provided before I ask.
- I have a solid foundation.
- I take great care of my body, mind and spirit.
- I love with my whole being.

- I know that I am protected, loved and valued.
- I have amazing friends and family.
- I care deeply for others.
- My light shines brightly for others to follow.
- My laughter is healing.
- Laughter is the healing this planet needs.
- I am the best person to get the word out about this experiment.
- My life is filled with great friends.
- I love to celebrate.
- I trust God.
- I am strong, confident and loving.
- I am funny, smart and sexy.

God's Vision or Message:

You are doing fabulously. I am so proud of you. You are living from your heart and sharing yourself with those you love without holding back. This is the way I designed you. You have such a capacity for love and lightness, yet so much of that gets clouded along the way and your lives become a searching to find your way back. The only issue you have is you spend your lives looking outside of yourself when you came in with everything you need to have everything you desire.

Coming from contribution and helping others is your greatest gift, Christiana. You have kept your innocence and trust even though you thought you lost it. I've always known what you are capable of. It's only a matter of time before you start fully understanding what I know to be true about you.

You are waking up to the truth of your potential, which has always been in your hands. The only thing that could and can ever stop you is you. That's the paradox. You are the most powerful creator. You have to power to manifest whatever you want and most of you manifest struggle and suffering. It's time you help wake people up. I need your help with this. You are a powerful woman and everything you've done thus far has prepared you for what's ahead. The fact that you are listening and taking action, enrolling others and sharing this message thus far is fact alone that you are the right person.

What is your vision of me with Dan?

He is a gift. Someone who sees you the way I see you. To remind you of who you really are. Enjoy your time with him and let yourself be happy. That is all I want for you, to be happy and know yourself fully. Let yourself love and be loved.

I worry that he doesn't want children.

Yes, I hear you. I told you your children are on their way. Trust me. It's all unfolding, as it should. You are worried that you'll write something that won't turn out and discredit this project in some way. Do not worry about such things. It's only a matter of time before you see how this plays out. This is your next big leap of faith. Trust that what you write will come through.

There is a part of you that is scared to really jump into a relationship. So in the past, you've chosen men who aren't available or who aren't able to receive you, which only proved to yourself what you feared: men aren't reliable.

You aren't the same person now. You are finding your way and Dan is a good man. With every relationship, there are parts you want and parts you don't. That only serves to guide you in your own development. What I love about him is how much he appreciates you. You are finally being with men that are more in alignment with who you truly are and support that vision of you.

Day 25 Exercise

Taking Stock:
What are 3 things/moments that take your breath away or have you pause with appreciation?

1._____
2._____
3._____

God's Belief System:
What are 3 things God would believe to be true about you?
Or you can use what he said for me?

1._____
2._____
3._____

What is God's vision or message for you?
Get still and listen for the voice or message. What is coming through?
Or what passage from my entry spoke to you?

Day 26: May 6, 2011

Taking Stock:

- I have the best people in my life
- The rays of sunlight filtering through my window
- A cup of tea in the morning
- Connecting with those I love
- Feeling love flow more easily through me
- Knowing I have amazing people around me
- I have the best friends
- The birds singing to me
- A hummingbird greeting me when I got home
- Sitting in a ray of sun
- The feel of summer in the air
- A smile from a stranger
- Connecting with a stranger
- Dancing
- Feeling love
- Feeling so full of energy I want to burst with happiness
- Feeling hopeful
- Believing in myself
- Trusting this process
- Committing to this process
- Coming from love
- Spending time with friends
- Dressing well and feeling good
- I love my life
- Helping people

God's Belief System:

- People are inherently good.
- I love myself.
- I take great care of my body, mind & spirit.

- The world is out for my highest good.
- I have heart-connected relationships with people.
- I love.
- I am happy, joyful, kind, trusting and funny.
- I am safe.
- I am blessed.
- People show me their best.
- I inspire people to take action in their lives.
- I'm doing what I'm supposed to be doing.

God's Vision or Message:

You are walking in the flow more now than ever. You feel this energy inside of you and you often times want to dull it down. Just breathe; it's your body assimilating to the new amounts of energy you are manifesting. You are supposed to be vibrating; that's how it goes. Tingling is good! Trust me. It's not about containing the energy rather riding the energy. Let it be you; you are it; it is all the same; it's all one.

You are a sexy, beautiful, dynamic woman. This is your time to shine and own that part of yourself you've been hiding from the world. You can't diminish one part of yourself and shine elsewhere... all of it must shine fully to fully embrace yourself. Compartmentalizing is an illusion. There isn't anything you can be that I haven't created. You must know contrast to decide who you want to be. There are no wrong choices. Just know that I support whatever you choose for yourself. You are strong, confident and yet there is that side that just wants someone to take care of you. You have always been taken care of; I've never left you. It's just a non-physical reality that you sometimes get challenged receiving. You deserve the best in life and from life.

Only you can decide how much of my bounty you are willing to receive. Crazy, isn't it, that you've been the gatekeeper this whole time? You are waking up to the truth of you and what you are capable of. This is good thing. You are listening and standing in my truth of you. This is a happy day for me that you've gotten behind this message and are spreading it. You have already helped many people on the path and the longer you are on the path the stronger you become and the stronger your faith in yourself and me. We are a team; I get to know myself through you and your choices. You can create such beauty or ugliness depending upon your vision. I don't see anything as ugly, rather only necessary for you to decide who you want to be. Yet you punish yourselves for choosing what you think to be wrong instead of embracing what feels right in your heart. You have so many rules about what something is supposed to look and feel like, that you limit what I can do through you based upon your belief system.

Fall in love with creating, experiencing and choosing what you want to be. Mistakes are how you all learn; there is no getting around it. Mistakes are gems and gifts to behold for they guide you to your path. There is no misery except what you choose to bring upon yourself. You have spent a great deal of your life beating yourself up. That voice in you for a long time has been stronger than my voice. You don't care for yourself or treat yourself gently. That voice is quite harsh; when that inner harsh voice acts up or speaks up, feel into your heart and if it doesn't lift your spirits see it for what it is, optional suffering. My only input is what lifts your spirit and raises your awareness and love. If it's not of that then it's not my vision of you.

Yes, everything is my creation. Contrast is necessary to experience this world. For if you know no other way, than you can't feel your experience or appreciate it for what it is. Feel the pulse the beating of your heart, that is my constant drumming to remind you that I am here with you at all times. While your heart is beating we are having this experience together. I'll never leave you. Always look inside yourself first for the truth of your own spirit. This is the beginning for you the source of your energy; trust it!

I see you beginning to feel your power settle into your body. This is good.

Day 26 Exercise

Taking Stock:
What are 3 things/moments that take your breath away or have you pause with appreciation?

1._____

2._____

3._____

God's Belief System:
What are 3 things God would believe to be true about you?
Or you can use what he said for me?

1._____

2._____

3._____

What is God's vision or message for you?
Get still and listen for the voice or message. What is coming through?
Or what passage from my entry spoke to you?

_____

_____

_____

_____

_____

_____

_____

_____

_____

_____

Day 27: May 7, 2011

Taking Stock:

- The birds are singing to me
- Going to see Terri play
- Going on a date with Dan
- My space heater warming my room taking out the chill
- My mom rooting for me
- Feeling how loved I am by everyone
- Showing how much I love those in my life
- Being moved to tears at the beauty of open heart communicating
- Seeing someone else shine
- Trusting myself
- My first 4 figure day
- My second 4 figure day
- Being flown out to organize a new client
- Being put up in a hotel
- Traveling
- Helping others get organized
- Helping others in general
- Creating more time with friends
- This process & what it's doing
- Right after a rain when the colors of foliage get brilliant, like in England

God's Belief System:

- I have the best friends.
- I love my life.
- Everyone is out to help me.
- People always show me their best.
- This process is helping others.
- My voice is meant to help others.
- I am an excellent speaker, trainer, presenter.

- The world is conspiring for my greatest good.
- My heart is open.
- How I love others is my healing and theirs.
- I am safe.
- I am blessed.
- My life is meant to help others wake up and lighten up.
- Laughter is healing this planet needs.
- I bring laughter wherever I go.
- I love teaching and training.
- I am ready to stand for this project.
- Everyday is an opportunity to make the world a better place.

God's Vision or Message:

Jude is opening you to the vision of what comes next.

I want to stay focused on finishing up the last days and setting the platform for what's to come next by handling the details that have been looming over me. It's so exciting how much money we generated in the last 7 days, yet it seems like after paying everything it's back to zero.

Watch your focus! You are on a generating pattern at the moment. You are doing great! I'm so proud of you. You are allowing yourself to receive. It's normal to have backlog to take care of. Just trust that it's all unfolding. More is coming and taking the actions you feel from me will be necessary to keep the gates open to receive. It's just your ego wanting to create suffering for you and take away your win. If it keeps you small, then it feels like you'll be safe. When in reality you are only suffering and it's taking a larger toll on your body than you are aware of. So many of you do this. You torture yourselves with focusing on what's not serving you and punishing yourself by reminding and paying more than once for something.

Mistakes are crucial to your development. They are not wrong, bad or ugly. They are just the opportunities to know what you want or don't want so you can choose what serves you better next time. This fascination with comparison feeds this dynamic. Have this or buy that to fill the holes that you think you have. I don't make holes or lack in anything I do. The feeling you are lacking anything comes from the belief that you are somehow less than worthy, are disconnected from me, or have to pay in some way to endear yourself to me. That isn't the truth. How could I create everything in the universe and then punish you for choosing something I created? It makes no sense. It's a good idea that has gotten out of control, in order to control. Yes, that is controversial. We are changing the dynamic together. There is nothing you need to do or place to go to connect with me. I'm here in every beat of your heart. Your heartbeat is your key to come back to me. It is our connection. I gave you something you could feel, a palpable connection a pulsing of life. This is our connection and you are a powerful creator.

You are becoming bolder and letting me speak without editing. I know you are concerned about what is coming out. You now know my heart and trust what you are hearing.

Each of you came into this life with all the answers from the beginning. You have an opportunity to know yourself in a way I cannot. I know myself through your experience. Live fully, risk your heart and trust me. You are doing this now. It's taking time to develop the muscle of trust and to develop the discipline that you are right where you need to be. You are also realizing you are getting more attention wherever you go, people are noticing you. You are radiating and they can feel the light. They are drawn to the light within you. Hold your heart open and be compassionate and know you are safe doing so. I know you fear when you are on stage that your energy will be depleted. When we have our connection going strong, there is no draining of your energy. No one can take that which is inherently yours especially if you are connected with me. There is no one that can truly ever harm you. It may look like that on the outside, yet it's simply not possible.

I only stand for love, joy, compassion, and laughter. Those things are all from me. Anything other than that is just a way to know you are out of alignment with me and to return to what feels good.

How can loving with an open heart be bad?

It isn't. You have so many rules on what things look like. You as culture hold these conversations to be truth for you. Yet if you look back over time, many adjustments have been made. The only truth you need to hold for yourself is what is in your highest good and makes your heart light up. You'll know and sense that it isn't in alignment that is when your wanting overrides your knowing. There is nothing wrong with that, just notice how are you feeling higher or lower... and adjust accordingly.

I don't judge you. I don't declare you must be one way or against me. I don't stop loving you if you do something you think I think is wrong. My love for you is and always has been unconditional. How can I not love a part of myself? How can I disown or deny a part of me? It's not possible.

I've sent you ideas that will help you stay connected with me. Somehow they've been turned into rules. It was just a path to follow if you wanted more harmony. You are exactly perfect. I know it's hard to believe. You are beautiful and lovely even when you are in pain. You still have such a beauty. I always am with you and reaching out to you. It's challenging to watch you suffer and struggle and think it's the way I want you to live. I wish only love, joy, abundance and lightness upon you. The rest isn't my desire. I forgive all you do. Truly there is nothing to forgive for it all comes from me.

You are challenging my listening now. It's getting too much.

No it's not... you are not wanting to take responsibility for this. You aren't the message.

What if I am wrong? What if?

You aren't, but what is wrong with challenging the way the culture is thinking. Twenty years from now you'll look back and think "Wow." Just like when you thought big hair and shoulder pads were all the rage. Now you look back and say, "What was I thinking?" That's the beauty of life, it's never the same; it's in constant motion and evolving moment-by-moment.

Yes, I hear you. Yes, I feel your heart. Every experience you have has gotten you here.

Day 27 Exercise

Taking Stock:
What are 3 things/moments that take your breath away or have you pause with appreciation?

1._____
2._____
3._____

God's Belief System:
What are 3 things God would believe to be true about you?
Or you can use what he said for me?

1._____
2._____
3._____

What is God's vision or message for you?
Get still and listen for the voice or message. What is coming through?
Or what passage from my entry spoke to you?

Day 28: May 8, 2011

Taking Stock:

- A great kiss
- Feeling good
- Sitting in the sunshine
- A hot tub
- Hanging out with friends
- Laughing
- Connecting with friends
- A great hug
- Cuddling
- My heater that warms my room
- A sweatshirt on a chilly night
- A smile from a stranger
- People helping me
- Being able to help other people
- When my friends feel like family
- Sharing this experiment
- Serendipity
- My shoulders getting rubbed
- A pedicure

God's Belief System:

- The world is a beautiful place.
- People always show me their best.
- I love helping people.
- I love my life.
- There is so much abundance in the world.
- My heart is open.
- My light shines brightly to guide others on their paths.
- I am strong, confident and funny.
- I am blessed.

- I am a powerful creator.
- I can create whatever I need or desire.
- I am successful at whatever I choose to focus on.
- This project is waking people up to our relationship.
- God is good.
- My life is blessed.
- I have the best friends and clients.
- My business is thriving.
- I root for other people to win.

God's Vision or Message:

You don't have to have everyone join you on this journey. We aren't looking for everyone and there isn't one way to get to me. This is your way and many others will use this as well. You also don't need validation from others; you know in your own body what value this process holds. So grab hold keep moving.

Today is a day of miracles. Did you see them?

Yes, free Starbucks.

That was the second. Opening up this morning was the first, when your reaction was fear and shut down. You risked asking a question and got the answer you were looking for. However, you had to walk through the fear to find the answer. That is life. Your head makes up fears and you must stand and walk through them, once you do you are free of it and then you can make better decisions. Everyone has moments of being unconscious so be gentle to everyone along this journey and be compassionate. Not everyone is aware of their actions, so gently remind them and remember you too have your moments. No one is what you consider perfect, therefore everyone would fare better to remember how awkward they used to be and come from a place of contribution and compassion.

Day 28 Exercise

Taking Stock:
What are 3 things/moments that take your breath away or have you pause with appreciation?

1._____
2._____
3._____

God's Belief System:
What are 3 things God would believe to be true about you?
Or you can use what he said for me?

1._____
2._____
3._____

What is God's vision or message for you?
Get still and listen for the voice or message. What is coming through?
Or what passage from my entry spoke to you?

_____
_____
_____
_____
_____
_____
_____
_____
_____
_____
_____

Day 29: May 9, 2001

Taking Stock:

- Feeling healthy
- Choosing my focus
- A great night's sleep
- The warmth of the sun
- My Cellerciser (a mini trampoline)
- A clean car
- The birds singing
- Spending time with friends
- Getting great news from Michael
- Reconnecting with old friends
- Falling in love
- Feeling my heart overflow with love
- Transforming an office in 1 day (organizing)
- Feeling at home in my body
- My connection with God
- This process
- Chicken soup
- A baked chicken dinner
- Spoiling my mom on mom's day
- Sharing my heart with my friends
- A heart connection with another person
- A great workout

God's Belief System:

- I choose my reality based on my thoughts.
- I can think myself healthy.
- I love my life.
- People are inherently good.
- I see the best in people.
- I meet the nicest people wherever I go.

- The world is conspiring for my good.
- My laughter is my healing.
- I bring out the best in others.
- I am blessed, loved, valued and adored.
- I have the best clients.
- I can be, do or have whatever I want.
- I am strong, confident and beautiful.
- I am fit, lean and healthy.
- I take great care of my body, mind and spirit.
- Helping others in need brings me great joy.

God's Vision or Message:

You are a powerful woman and creator. You have transformed your experience. Trust that it is exactly perfect and you are right. You choose your reality, as you'd like to live it. Though many aren't conscious they are controlling their experiences. So they are creating their lives through default.

What a great day for you. I love that you embraced the day and decided to make it your own and chose how you would live it. You can keep this short tonight you are doing great. I'm so proud of you. You were getting run down a bit and your desire to connect was a bit stronger than your desire to take care of yourself. Just notice and make adjustments. All is perfect! You are doing great. Keep it up.

I know your heart. You are fine. You are exceeding your own expectations. I know you don't believe that even though you are. You are sticking with this process, transforming your business, relationships, quality of your life, and strength of spirit and connection with me. You believe in yourself more than ever and you are a great love. We are only scratching the surface.

Rest now; you need that more than what we are discussing and listen to your inner guidance and follow its instructions.

Day 29 Exercise

Taking Stock:
What are 3 things/moments that take your breath away or have you pause with appreciation?

1._____
2._____
3._____

God's Belief System:
What are 3 things God would believe to be true about you?
Or you can use what he said for me?

1._____
2._____
3._____

What is God's vision or message for you?
Get still and listen for the voice or message. What is coming through?
Or what passage from my entry spoke to you?

Day 30: May 10, 2011

Taking Stock:

- Having the freedom to play hooky and go to Disneyland today
- Getting a free pass to Disneyland
- Bouncing on my Cellerciser
- Going on a date
- Holding hands
- Riding roller coasters
- Riding tea cups
- Watching children play, squeal and laugh
- People watching
- Being able to share what's on my mind
- The trees blowing in the wind
- Hummingbirds
- The light of the setting sun
- A sweatshirt on a cold night
- A hot shower
- A cup of tea
- A kiss on the forehead
- Feeling love in my heart overflow
- A great kiss

God's Belief System:

- The world is out for my good.
- I have the best friends in the world.
- Abundance is everywhere I look.
- Laughter is healing, my laughter is my healing.
- People are inherently good.
- I see the light in people.
- Every day is an opportunity to make the world a better place.
- I am blessed, loved, valued and adored.
- Miracles happen every day.

- It's the small moments that matter most.
- The world is full of beauty, love and joy.
- There is something beautiful in each and every person.
- We are all connected.
- By loving others, I love myself.
- I see the best in others.
- I am walking my path.

God's Vision or Message:

This process has me in a very heart open space. I'm able to easily express how I'm feeling moment by moment.

Yes, that is how this works. We are in constant connection. Trust in the process of your life unfolding and watch out for miracles along the way. Keep your attention firmly upon what you are wanting and release attachment to how it shows up. You will naturally attract what it is you are wanting, even though it may not come in the package or the way you believe it will. Give me room to show up for you. There is so much more I can do through you; don't limit me by putting your expectations on things.

Look back over your life and remember how many times things turned out bigger or better than you expected. I'm always sending you abundance in every aspect of your life. Don't get attached to where it's coming from; you'll miss out on what's right in front of you.

Now you are gaining a deeper understanding of how big this little project is. You are seeing how people are going to get their power back and remember who they are and what they are here for. It's always the simple things that yield the grandest results.

I love the way you share your heart. You have given yourself over to this process. You are remarkable in every way. You bring me such joy watching the way you live your life and reach out to me throughout this process. This gift you are bringing to others is a simple thing with massive results. You are taking out the middleman by communicating with me directly. You are also adjusting the process and belief around communicating with me. Thank you.

Everyone has the ability to reach me and hear me. It's your birthright, everyone's birthright. It has always been my wish to have open communication with you. I'm always here, yet with this experiment you are helping others develop their listening too.

Can you imagine a world with so many self-empowered people who are all waking up to my vision of their life? It's exponential the ripple effect. This is the best possible outcome for our time together bridging that gap.

Here we are together on day 30. You've stuck with me all month. So how do you feel?

I'm more grounded. My underlying anxiousness and fear are gone. My relationships are richer and my heart is more open. My business is taking off. I love the possibility opening up. I feel valuable, trust my value and ability to deliver what I say I will. I'm no longer looking outside of myself for answers. I have an inner strength that isn't wavering. I feel amazing. Everything doesn't even need to go my way for me to feel that way either. Thank you.

This is going to shift the paradigm; it's going to wake people up to the truth of themselves. It's going to help people focus their attention inward and get answers from that place, their inner knowing and that still small voice within, me. You'll see this start slowly and then mushroom. This is just another aspect of you organizing people's lives, just a variation of it. You are showing people their way, their truth but having them discover it for themselves. No have tos, shoulds, or work involved; rather show up and see if your life changes, see what God thinks is possible for you. See if by chance he could be right.

Is this just going to be a way of life with us?

Yes, it always has been a way of life, you just weren't aware of it fully. Now you are experiencing our connection in a deeper way. You have much ahead of you. Stay in communication with me. It can take on a different structure now that we are connected. If you ever feel you lose our connection, just come back to this practice and start again. I will be here waiting for you. I am always here, just like the beating of your heart. As long as your heart beats, know that I am walking right beside you and we are in this together.

Day 30 Exercise

Taking Stock:
What are 3 things/moments that take your breath away or have you pause with appreciation?

1._____
2._____
3._____

God's Belief System:
What are 3 things God would believe to be true about you?
Or you can use what he said for me?

1._____
2._____
3._____

What is God's vision or message for you?
Get still and listen for the voice or message. What is coming through?
Or what passage from my entry spoke to you?

About the Author

It has been said that our childhood determines who we become.

I've been a teacher ever since I can remember. It started in preschool around age 3, as my mom remembers. My father made me a homemade chalkboard with an easel. I would come home each day and reteach my mom, the animals and my stuffed animals everything I learned that day. It's taken many shapes and forms over the years.

I grew up in a small town in western Massachusetts, Greenfield. I was a young girl with a big imagination. My father groomed me with personal development from a young age. Not fitting the traditional work model, I've been an entrepreneur since 1997. For the last 20 years I've been an Organizational and Strategic Planning Consultant. I love helping people bring their ideas to life: finding the structure, flow and order.

When I was young, I spent 10 years waiting to be rescued, then 15 years rescuing others, for the last 10 years I realized if I help people see their own value, then they don't need to be rescued. It's been my passion to help others get clear on their message, value, and how they want to deliver it.

Additionally, since 2010, I've been an Assistant Trainer and Trainer in the U.S. and internationally with Peak Potentials, New Peaks and Success Resources. It's been my greatest pleasure inspiring people to reach for their dreams and fulfill their potential.

At no point in my life did I think I would be the person to write a book about God. I have resisted and avoiding putting this book out for many years. The journal was actually written back in 2011.

You know that critical voice inside your head, the one that says, "Who do you think you are?" My voice was very loud and very strong. It kept saying, "You are not the best example. Look at your life. You've made mistakes. You don't go to church regularly. You resist joining communities. You've failed so many times. What makes you think you have the right to say anything or lead anyone anywhere?" I asked God and he said, "You are the perfect person for exactly that reason." I choose to believe him.